ADVANTAGE Reading

4

Table of Contents

Table of Contents

CREDITS

Concept Development: Kent Publishing Services, Inc.
Written by: Robbie Butler
Editor: Carla Hamaguchi
Designer/Production: Moonhee Pak/Terri Lamadrid
Illustrators: Frank Ordaz and Corbin Hillam
Art Director: Tom Cochrane
Project Director: Carolea Williams

Introduction

The Advantage Reading Series for grades 3–6 is shaped and influenced by current research findings in literacy instruction grounded in the federally mandated *No Child Left Behind* Act. It includes the following key skill strands:

- phonics/structural word analysis
- vocabulary development
- reading fluency
- reading comprehension

This series offers strong skill instruction along with motivational features in an easy-to-use format.

Take a look at all the advantages this reading series offers . . .

Phonics/Structural Word Analysis

Word analysis activities include the study of word syllabication, prefixes, suffixes, synonyms, antonyms, word roots, similes, metaphors, idioms, adjectives, adverbs, and much more. Word analysis helps students increase their **vocabulary, word-recognition skills,** and **spelling skills.**

Variety of Reading Genres

Fiction and Nonfiction

Students will have many opportunities to build reading skills by reading a variety of fiction, nonfiction, and poetry selections created in a **variety of visual formats** to simulate authentic reading styles. Each story selection builds on content vocabulary and skills introduced in the section. Fiction selections include fantasy, legends, realistic fiction, first-person narratives, and poetry. Nonfiction selections include biographies, how-to's, reports, and directions.

Graphic Information

Graphic information reading selections include charts, graphs, labels, maps, diagrams, and recipes. These types of reading opportunities help students hone **real-life reading** skills.

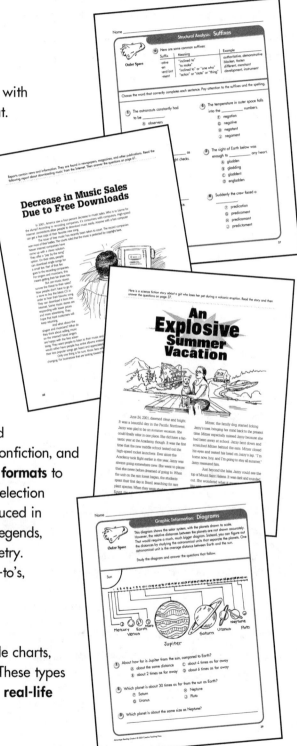

Comprehension Strategies

Strategic comprehension activities encourage students to make connections, ask questions, make predictions, and think about strategies they can use to **increase their understanding** of the text's meaning.

Fluency Practice

Reading fluency is the ability to **read with expression,** intonation, and a natural flow that sounds like talking. Fluency is essential for comprehension because the lack of it results in choppy, robotic reading that stands in the way of making sense out of a phrase or sentence.

Writing

Reading and writing are partner skills. A **range of writing activities** helps students improve their ability to write as well as learn about different forms of writing, such as signs, notes, personal narratives, riddles, poems, descriptions, journals, stories, and friendly letters.

Extensions and Real-Life Applications

Each unit ends with a "More Things to Do" page that includes suggestions for **hands-on experiences** that extend the theme. A list of books is also included for further study and enjoyment of the unit's theme.

Answer Key

Answers for each page are provided at the back of the book to make **checking answers quick and easy.**

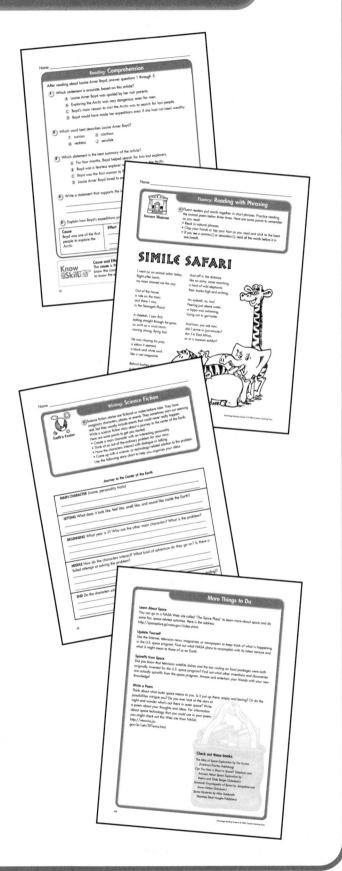

Name _____

My America

Where in the United States do you live?
Write the name of your state in the correct region on the chart below.
Write one state in each of the regions on the chart.

Town or City _____   State   _____

County   _____

Northeast	Southeast	Midwest	Southwest	West
Connecticut	Alabama	Illinois	Arizona	Alaska
Delaware	Arkansas	Indiana	New Mexico	California
Maine	Florida	Iowa	Oklahoma	Colorado
Maryland	Georgia	Kansas	Texas	Hawaii
Massachusetts	Kentucky	Michigan		Idaho
New Hampshire	Louisiana	Minnesota		Montana
New Jersey	Mississippi	Missouri		Nevada
New York	North Carolina	Nebraska		Oregon
Pennsylvania	South Carolina	North Dakota		Utah
Rhode Island	Tennessee	Ohio		Washington
Vermont	Virginia	South Dakota		Wyoming
	West Virginia	Wisconsin		

Name _____

My America

Phonics: Long and Short Vowel Review

⭐ A **syllable** is a word or word part that contains a vowel. The vowels are *a, e, i, o, u,* and sometimes *y*. In every syllable, you will find a vowel. Below are some examples of short and long vowels. Note that the same vowel sound can be spelled in different ways.

Short Vowel Sounds	Long Vowel Sounds
cat	tape, day, rain
egg	see, sea, scene
pin	pine, night, skies
hot	note, coat, oh
cup	cube, you, unit

Sort the words by the first vowel sound. Write the words whose first vowel sound is short in the Short Vowel box. Write the words whose first vowel sound is long in the Long Vowel box.

cake	by	head	summer	spring	box	oat
shell	apple	rock	bleed	nose	kind	tube

Short Vowel

1 _____
2 _____
3 _____
4 _____
5 _____
6 _____
7 _____

Long Vowel

8 _____
9 _____
10 _____
11 _____
12 _____
13 _____
14 _____

Advantage Reading Grade 4 © 2004 Creative Teaching Press

Phonics: Long Vowel Review

My America

This lesson will teach you some of the ways to spell the long vowel sounds. In each word, underline the letters that make the long vowel sound. Then write another word that spells that long vowel sound the same way.

Long a Words

1 cupcake _____

2 mailbox _____

3 payoff _____

4 neighborhood _____

Long e Words

5 teacup _____

6 sweetheart _____

Long i Words

7 campfire _____

8 diehard _____

9 highchair _____

10 butterfly _____

Long o Words

11 toenail _____

12 rainbow _____

13 billfold _____

14 sailboat _____

15 undertone _____

16 overrun _____

Long u Words

17 fruitcake _____

18 flashcube _____

Phonics: **Long Vowel Review**

My America

Each numbered word below has a long vowel sound. Say the word, then write one word that rhymes with it. The first one is done as an example.

Long a Words

1 reign _____brain_____

2 nail _____

3 way _____

4 state _____

Long i Words

10 sky _____

11 right _____

12 find _____

13 tried _____

Long e Words

5 meter _____

6 baby _____

7 east _____

8 tree _____

9 piece _____

Long o Words

14 vote _____

15 coast _____

16 ocean _____

17 grow _____

Long u Words

18 true _____

19 tune _____

Advantage Reading Grade 4 © 2004 Creative Teaching Press

Name _____

My America

⭐ Remember that a syllable is a word or word part that contains a vowel. Every syllable has one vowel sound only, even though that sound may be spelled with more than one vowel. Some words have one syllable, and others have more.

One-Syllable Words	Two-Syllable Words
vote	voter
state	statement
rain	weather
turn	return

Underline the one-syllable words in the sentences below. Circle the words that have more than one syllable.

1 Groups of states make up the five regions of the United States.

2 The states in a region share similar features, such as landforms, climate, resources, and vegetation.

Underline the one-syllable words in the state names below.

3 Georgia, New York, Ohio, California, Maine, West Virginia

4 Texas, New Hampshire, Rhode Island, North Dakota, South Carolina

Structural Analysis: **Syllabication**

My America

⭐ Each syllable has only one vowel sound. The letter or letters that make up that sound may stand alone (o/pen, ei/ther) or may be joined by one or more consonants (mul/ti/ply, aunt).

You can divide some words into syllables by splitting the word between two consonants: rep/tile, run/ner, hit/ter, bas/ket.

However, some groups of consonants always stay together: bed/spread, tooth/brush, night/shirt, church/yard.

Draw slash lines between the letters (let/ters) to break these words into syllables. Four of these words are not compound words. Circle these four words.

1 milkshake	**2** playground	**3** football
4 hamburger	**5** market	**6** teenage
7 chipmunk	**8** legal	**9** nightgown
10 bathrobe	**11** impress	**12** overthrow

Advantage Reading Grade 4 © 2004 Creative Teaching Press

Fluency: Reading for Accuracy

My America

⭐ Below is a radio ad for a vacation area in the Southeast. Pretend you are an actor who will be reading this ad on the radio. Think about these things as you practice reading the ad at least three times:

• Make sure you understand what the text means.
• Pronounce all words clearly.
• Use a friendly tone of voice.
• Moderate the pace and tempo of your speech to fit the message.
• Use pauses or slow down your speech to stress key points.
• Make it interesting for the listener.

When you are ready, have a friend listen to you read the ad. Ask about ways to improve your speaking. When you are happy with your delivery, read the ad to a group of your classmates.

 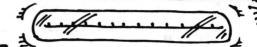

Birds head south; so should you! Why visit coastal Georgia in winter? The Low Country's mild weather means year-round sports. With so many sunny days, you'll think it's summer. Choose from tennis, golf, horse riding, or beach walking. Historic sites offer family fun, too. And then there is the food!

In coastal Georgia, you can step into the past. St. Catherine's Island's ruined Spanish mission dates from 1586. In 1733, the English founded Savannah. Its leafy squares boast grand 18th and 19th century homes. Explore historic Fort Pulaski on the Cockspur Islands. Tybee Island has Fort Screven. There is also Fort Frederica on Saint Simons Island.

As well as history, you'll find tasty seafood. A famous Low Country dish is Brunswick stew. There's pecan pie for dessert. Your hosts will say, "Y'all come back now!" I bet you will!

Name _____

Reading: **Comprehension**

After reading the ad on page 11, answer questions 1 through 5.

1 Read the first paragraph of the radio ad on the previous page. In your own words, write on the lines the main idea, that is, the most important thing the ad tells you.

_____

_____

_____

2 What is the ad telling you about this topic?

_____

_____

_____

3 In the first paragraph, the ad gives four reasons for visiting coastal Georgia. Write those four reasons.

_____

_____

_____

_____

4 In your own words, summarize what the ad says about each of these four reasons.

_____

_____

_____

_____

5 Are you convinced? Would you want to go to coastal Georgia? Give one reason why or why not.

_____

_____

_____

_____

Vocabulary: **Frequently Confused Words**

My America

⭐ Some words are often spelled incorrectly because they look or sound almost alike. Computer spelling checks do not flag these words as misspelled because they are not misspelled, they are just misused. The only way to avoid mixing these words up is to know how to spell them and to check your writing to be sure you have used the right word in the right way.

Read each pair of sentences. Circle the words with the same, or nearly the same, sound.

1 My parents say the Northeast is their favorite region of the United States.
We are going back there this summer.

2 My grandparents still live there.
They're looking forward to my visit.

3 There's my grandparents' house in the photo.
The big dog next to the porch is theirs.

4 Last time we drove through the night to get there because we got lost.
My baby brother threw the map out of the window.

5 When we're through with it, Mom wants to look at the map to plan the route.
Such a long trip takes thorough planning.

6 You're welcome to come with us.
Will your parents let you?

Read each sentence. Choose one of the pair of words to complete each sentence. Write the word on the line.

7 You seem happy about _____ family's plans for the summer.
(you're, your)

8 The places in the West that _____ planning to visit should be fun.
(you're, your)

9 Take pictures of some of the animals that you see _____.
(their, there)

Vocabulary: **Content Words**

My America

⭐ In daily life, certain words are most often used in certain situations. When you are traveling, finding your way, or giving directions, certain words come up over and over. Words that tell you "where" are sometimes called **directional** words. These words are often used in geography lessons.

Read the sentences. The words in bold are directional words.

• We flew **over** the mountains, and then the plane headed **north.**
• The train does not stop **between** New York and Washington.
• You turn **right** and then drive **under** the bridge.
• The hotel is **in front of** the park, which **is across from** the train station.
• Drive to the parking lot **behind** the store **opposite** the school.

Read the following sentences and circle each directional word. You may circle more than one word in some sentences.

1 To find the museum, turn left at the library.

2 You must pay for your tickets at the counter near the south gate.

3 In the middle of the town, you can find many hotels.

4 Most of the best restaurants are inside the city limits.

5 Below the equator, June is the middle of winter.

6 Above the equator, December is the middle of winter.

7 My cousins live beyond the city limits to the southeast of town.

8 The bus drove alongside the train tracks for miles.

Advantage Reading Grade 4 © 2004 Creative Teaching Press

The Native American Midwest

The Midwest covers a vast area. In the region's western part, the Great Plains stretch across some 400 miles wide. To the north and the east lie the Great Lakes. From these flow the many rivers that make the eastern, middle, and southern parts of the region so green and fertile. The dry, windy Great Plains differ from the lush, green river valley forests. So life on the plains contrasted with life near the rivers.

For many centuries, huge buffalo herds lived on the Great Plains. From before the 1500s, the tribes that hunted the buffalo also lived on the plains. In the Midwest of the late 1700s were many Plains tribes. These included the Arapaho, Cheyenne, Comanche, and Sioux. For tribes like the Sioux, life focused on the buffalo. They slept in buffalo hide tipis. The Sioux's daily food, clothes, and tools came from the buffaloes they hunted. Following the herds, the Sioux moved from place to place across the northern plains. They moved up and down both sides of the Missouri River.

Native Americans did not live only on the Great Plains. They lived all over the Midwest. By the 1600s, in what is now Michigan, tribes included the Chippewa, Menominee, Ottawa, Huron, Potawatomi, and Miami. The Shawnee, Delaware, and Wyandot lived in what is now Ohio.

While the Plains tribes lived a nomadic life, other midwestern tribes stayed put. Many settled along the rivers in the forests of the central, southern, and eastern parts of the region. Like the Sioux, the Miami were hunters. Unlike the Sioux, the Miami also farmed. They made homes along the Ohio and other smaller rivers. Because rivers and rainfall made these valleys fertile, the Sioux grew crops. They felled trees to make fields. There they grew corn, beans, and squash. They made villages in the forest near their fields. Men, women, and children gathered nuts and berries from the forest. They gathered food, they grew food, and they killed food. From the forest, they also took wood and bark. With this, they made wigwams and canoes. The canoes meant they could fish the rivers as well as farm the land and hunt the forest. By the 1700s, the villages and farms of the river valley tribes had been established for generations.

Reading: Comprehension

After reading *The Native American Midwest* on page 15, answer questions 1 through 3.

1 Why did so many Native American tribes live in the Great Plains?

- Ⓐ They could fish in the many lakes and rivers.
- Ⓑ They could live off the buffalo that roamed the plains in great herds.
- Ⓒ They could grow corn in the wet, rainy weather of the Great Plains.
- Ⓓ They could not leave because they had no boats.

2 The passage says that the Sioux lived a nomadic life. What does the word *nomadic* mean?

- Ⓕ moving from place to place
- Ⓖ moving only when forced by floods to move
- Ⓗ living in one place for a long period of time
- Ⓙ living in the mountains until the snow came

3 Complete the Venn diagram by filling in the blank spaces.

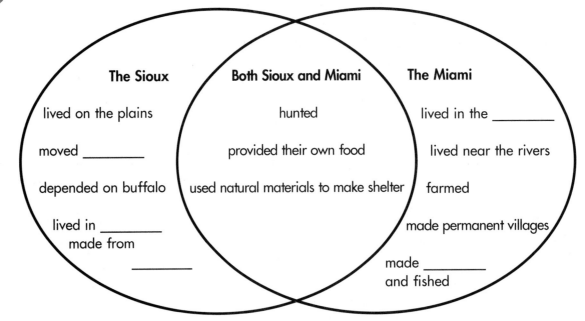

The Sioux

lived on the plains

moved _____

depended on buffalo

lived in _____
made from

_____

Both Sioux and Miami

hunted

provided their own food

used natural materials to make shelter

The Miami

lived in the _____

lived near the rivers

farmed

made permanent villages

made _____
and fished

Compare and Contrast
To compare and contrast two things, think about how they are alike and how they are different. A Venn diagram can help you compare and contrast. It helps you see how two things differ and how they are the same.

          Advantage Reading Grade 4 © 2004 Creative Teaching Press

Historical fiction takes place in the past. Some historical fiction uses real places and real events. The characters may or may not have been real people. The following fictional letter describes a Texas cattle drive from San Antonio to Abilene, Kansas, in 1871. The letter writer, Jason Jarman, is the main character and also the narrator. Jason is 14 years old, and this is his first cattle drive. While the people and events are imaginary, the author includes many real facts about life on a cattle drive. Read the letter and then answer the questions on pages 20–21.

Dear Jessica,

What's happening in Atlanta? I bet you're being invited to birthday parties and tea parties every week! Well, life on this cattle drive is a bit different. I still can't believe Dad and Uncle Horace let me come. Your last letter asked me dozens of questions. I'll try to answer them by telling you a bit about what we're doing.

You know Uncle Horace always complains about how tough cattle ranching can be. And Dad always laughs since Uncle Horace is so rich. Well, remember what Uncle H. always says about cattle ranching? He says the hardest part is getting cattle to the slaughterhouses in Chicago so the meat can be sold to butchers' shops around the country. Well, he's right. I'm not going to laugh at him anymore.

Before Uncle H. and I left Atlanta and got to the ranch, the cowboys had rounded up 2,400 cattle. The cowboys were worn out from the roundup. It took them weeks to gather the cattle from the open plains and herd them into pens. They had a day to rest before this cattle drive began. We have to take 2,400 cattle to the trains at Abilene. That's over 500 miles. We follow the Chisholm Trail, so at least everyone but me has been here before and knows the way. Getting lost is about the only thing we don't have to worry about.

We get up before dawn every morning. The cook drives the chuck wagon, a kitchen on wheels, and he has to leave way ahead of us so he can get to the next stopping point before us. He has to get the chuck wagon set up and get lunch cooked before we catch up with him. Then he does the same thing to get dinner ready for our evening stop. I help him make the coffee each morning.

We eat pancakes and beans, sometimes along with salt pork and biscuits. And we drink tons of coffee. The cook puts lots of molasses in the coffee to cover up the bitter taste. The cowboys call him Cookie, or sometimes Sugar, because of the sweet coffee. Get it? Sugar Cookie? After breakfast, things get tough.

The trail boss assigned me to work with the wrangler. A wrangler is a sort of junior cowboy who has to look after the remuda, the herd of extra horses. So I'm a sort of junior assistant cowboy, the lowest of the low. Since I love horses, I don't mind. The wrangler's name is Kit, and he's only 17. He's really great. Kit and I herd the remuda as far away from the cowboys and the cattle as we can. If we ever get stuck behind them, we eat dust all day long. Even if I tie my new red bandanna over my nose and mouth, it doesn't keep the dust and dirt out. It's really hard to breathe in clouds of dust. I never thought I could grow to hate dust and dirt so much. Mom will be glad to hear that I wish I could take a bath every day!

Last night something scary happened. We'd just finished our beef stew with potatoes and even more beans. We were drinking our coffee when a mountain lion attacked one of the youngest steers. Within seconds, the cowboys had their guns

Advantage Reading Grade 4 © 2004 Creative Teaching Press

out, and the trail boss shot the mountain lion. Now, the worst thing that can happen on a drive is a stampede. If the cattle get frightened, they will just start running. Think how hard it would be to stop 2,400 cattle, each weighing hundreds of pounds. The boss had to kill the lion with one shot. More shots would have started a stampede for sure.

We had to get ready to move fast in case the herd started to stampede. But after awhile, the boss said he thought they had settled down. Then we heard something and saw three shapes moving near the dead mountain lion. Some of us went to investigate. Three baby mountain lions were crying for their mother. You know how I feel about animals. The cubs were so cute. It seems I'm not the only one who has a soft spot. Before long, even the toughest cowboy was playing with the cubs. The boss said we should shoot them, but he couldn't bring himself to do it.

One of the cowboys, Nathan, an ex-slave, lived in the mountains for a time after he ran away from his owners. He spent months watching and studying the mountain lions while he was in hiding. He said that if we left the cubs enough to eat for a few days, they might survive. Sugar Cookie turned out to be a real sweetie after all. He took three huge chunks of beef from the chuck wagon. Then Kit, Nathan, and I carried the cubs until we found a creek by a rocky hillside. Behind some rocks we found a small, cave-like hole in the hill. We put the cubs and the beef in there. I hope they make it.

It's time for bed. I'll try to write again in a day or two. Think about me as you enjoy your peach ice cream, pecan pie, and hot baths.

With love from your extremely tired and very dirty big brother,

Jason

Name _____

Reading: Comprehension

After reading the letter on pages 17 through 19, answer questions 1 through 11.

1 What is a *remuda*?

_____

_____

2 What is a *wrangler*?

    Ⓕ   a snake that wraps itself around you and squeezes you to death

    Ⓖ   a horse that has not been trained to carry a rider

    Ⓗ   a type of saddle that wraps tightly around the horse

    Ⓙ   a less-experienced cowboy who is in charge of the remuda

3 Who is telling about the cattle drive?

    Ⓐ   the letter writer, Jason Jarman

    Ⓑ   a girl named Jessica in Atlanta

    Ⓒ   an ex-slave named Nathan

    Ⓓ   Kit, the wrangler

4 Why are they driving the cattle to Abilene?

    Ⓕ   to sell them at the annual cattle market and fair

    Ⓖ   to put them on the train to go to the Chicago slaughterhouses

    Ⓗ   to train the cattle to travel in herds and not stampede

    Ⓙ   to make the cattle tired so they will be easy to herd

5 Why does the cook leave the campsite each morning before the cowboys?

_____

_____

6 Why does Jason tell his sister to think about him while she enjoys peach ice cream, pecan pie, and hot baths?

_____

_____

Advantage Reading Grade 4 © 2004 Creative Teaching Press

Reading: **Comprehension**

7 Why is it important that the trail boss only shot once?

    Ⓐ He had only one bullet and no more.

    Ⓑ Cattle rustlers might hear the shots and come to steal the cattle.

    Ⓒ Loud noises frighten the cattle and might make them stampede.

    Ⓓ If he were a bad shot, the men would not respect him.

8 Why had the cowboy named Nathan once spent time hiding in the mountains?

    Ⓕ He was a mountain climber and an explorer who was looking for a new mountain pass.

    Ⓖ He was a bank robber and gunslinger, wanted dead or alive.

    Ⓗ He was hiding from mountain lions, which had been following him.

    Ⓙ He was a runaway slave.

9 List four things Jason likes.

_____

_____

10 Jason tells his sister what he knows and feels about several of the characters. Do any of the other characters in the story tell you anything at all about Jason? Why?

_____

_____

11 List three things you like about Jason. Are there any things you don't like about Jason? What are they?

_____

_____

Analyzing Characters
In order to understand a character in a story, you need to look at four things: what the character thinks, what she or he does, what the character says, and what other characters or the narrator tell you about the character.

Graphic Information: **Time Line**

My America

 History books, especially textbooks, often use time lines to help readers understand and remember the order in which events occurred.

Use the vertical time line below to answer the questions.

California Before Statehood: Important Dates in California's Past

1500s	Some 300,000 Native Americans live in California.
1542	Employed by Spain, Juan Rodríguez Cabrillo, a Portuguese sailor, explores San Diego Bay.
1769	Near what is now San Diego, Junípero Serra establishes the first Franciscan mission.
1822	The new Mexican government, newly independent from Spain, begins to govern California, now part of Mexico.
1841	The first wagon train of U.S. settlers arrives in California.
1848	After the Mexican War, Mexico gives up California to the United States.
1848	Gold is discovered at Sutter's Mill near San Francisco, and the gold rush begins.
1849	Thousands of prospectors, called "forty-niners," come to California in search of gold.
1850	On September 9, California becomes the 31st state.

1 Which came first: the gold rush or the Spanish missions?

_____

2 Who first lived in California?

_____

3 Why were the California gold rush prospectors called "forty-niners"?

_____

4 For how many years did Mexico govern California?

_____

 Advantage Reading Grade 4 © 2004 Creative Teaching Press

Writing: **Writing to Persuade**

My America

⭐ When a writer writes to persuade a reader to do something, the writer must plan his or her arguments carefully. Effective persuasive writing includes more facts than opinions. The facts should be used to support the arguments the writer makes. The better the examples and facts a writer presents, the more likely the reader is to be persuaded.

Choose the part of the United States you like most. Then plan and write a persuasive argument that explains why people should visit this part of the United States during their vacation this year.

Use the graphic organizer below to plan your persuasive argument. Write the name of the region or place you will write about, and write some ideas about how you will introduce your arguments. Give at least two reasons with at least one supporting fact or example for each reason.

Why You Should Vacation in _____ This Year

Introduction (How I'll begin)

_____
_____

Reason 1	Reason 2	Reason 3	Other thoughts and opinions
_____	_____	_____	_____
_____	_____	_____	_____
_____	_____	_____	_____
_____	_____	_____	_____
_____	_____	_____	_____
_____	_____	_____	_____
_____	_____	_____	_____
_____	_____	_____	_____

Conclusion (How I'll summarize my argument)

_____
_____

Write your persuasive argument on the lines below. Use the notes you made in the graphic organizer on page 23.

_____

_____

_____

_____

_____

_____

_____

_____

_____

_____

_____

_____

_____

_____

Have a friend read your persuasive argument. Ask your friend which part he or she found most convincing. Was your friend persuaded?

Word Practice

Look at the words on page 8. With a partner, take turns reading the words aloud. See how many compound words you can make by adding another word before or after the numbered word.

Speech Practice

Reread the ad on page 11. Notice how at the beginning the writer tells you the main idea of the ad. The writer also tells the listeners/readers the key points that she will make. This helps the listeners/readers understand and remember these key points.

Write a short speech on one of these topics. Tell your listeners/readers what your main idea is, or what your speech will be about. Then tell them the two to four main or key points you will make.

• How to choose a vacation spot.
• Why I would or would not like to go on a cattle drive of the 1800s.
• The Native Americans of the _____ region of the United States.
• Why I do or do not like to vacation at the beach.

Travel Plans Notebook

Make a travel plans notebook for a trip you would like to take to a region of the United States. Make a section for each of the places you would like to visit and the sights you would like to see. Include photographs or drawings, or pictures cut from old magazines or travel brochures. Add a caption for each picture. Share your notebook with a parent or other adult.

Check out these books.

American Folk Songs for Children by Ruth Crawford Seeger (Music Sales Corporation)
By the Great Horn Spoon! by Sid Fleischman (Little, Brown and Company)
Dakota Dugout by Ann Warren Turner (Aladdin)
Dragonwings by Laurence Yep (HarperTrophy)
Journey Home by Yoshiko Uchida (Scott Foresman/Pearson K–12)
Little House on the Prairie by Laura Ingalls Wilder (HarperColllins)
My Prairie Year by Brett Harvey (Holiday House)
Sarah Plain and Tall by Patricia MacLachlan (HarperCollins)

Name _____

Deep in the Ocean

Oceans cover 71% of the surface of Earth. From the seashore, the bottom of the ocean slopes down, bit by bit. As the ocean bottom falls away, the water gets deeper and deeper. Different sorts of animals live at different depths of the ocean.

If you could walk or swim from the shore down into the deepest depths of the ocean, what do you think you would see along the way? In the web below, list some things that you might see in each part of the ocean. List living things and other sights you might see.

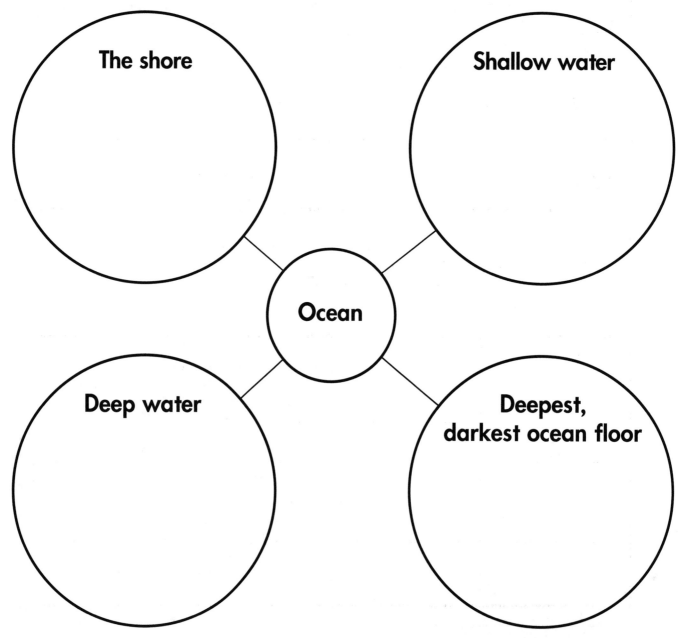

The shore

Shallow water

Ocean

Deep water

Deepest, darkest ocean floor

Advantage Reading Grade 4 © 2004 Creative Teaching Press

Phonics: **Consonant Blends**

Deep in the Ocean

 When two or more consonants appear together, they often spell a sound known as a consonant blend. The sounds of the two consonants blend together. Below are four groups of consonant blends. Say the words and listen carefully to the beginning sounds.

Consonant Blends

r blends	brave	crow	drop	fry	grow	prove	train
l blends	blue	clean	flower	glow	play	slip	
s blends	scout	skip	small	snore	spot	stove	sweep
3-letter blends	scrape	throw	shred	squirrel	spray	split	strike

Write four other words for each consonant blend category on the lines below. Use the consonant blend list above to think of other words that are NOT on the list.

r blends	l blends	s blends	3 letter blends
_____	_____	_____	_____
_____	_____	_____	_____
_____	_____	_____	_____
_____	_____	_____	_____

Phonics: **Consonant Blends**

Deep in the Ocean

 Some consonant blends can appear within a word.

Consonant Blends within a Word

cyclone	laundry	bugler	describe
oblige	secret	regret	asleep
cobra	afloat	replay	patrol
asked	inspire	apron	between

Write the consonant blend within each word on the line.

1. rollerskate _____
2. escape _____
3. despite _____
4. poster _____
5. tablet _____
6. reclaim _____
7. inflate _____
8. wiggly _____
9. deploy _____

10. nonslip _____
11. algebra _____
12. decree _____
13. undress _____
14. Africa _____
15. degree _____
16. April _____
17. waitress _____
18. untwist _____

Name _____

Phonics: Consonant Blends

Deep in the Ocean

★ Some consonant blends appear only in the middle or at the end of a word. These blends never appear at the beginning of a word. Here are some examples:
ra**ng**, si**ng**er, so**ck**, pi**ck**ed, si**nk**, ba**nk**ing.

Read each word. Write a word that rhymes with it.

1 hang _____

2 linger _____

3 deck _____

4 locker _____

5 hunk _____

6 winking _____

Read each sentence out loud. Circle the word that has a consonant blend at the beginning and at the end. Then write the word on the line.

7 She broke the clasp on her necklace. _____

8 That pink flower would be perfect if it did not stink. _____

9 The seal was very strong. _____

10 The clock sank into the sea. _____

11 Mom always takes a brisk walk after dinner. _____

12 Do not twist the fabric. _____

Name _____

Structural Analysis: VC/CV Syllabication Rule

Deep in the Ocean

⭐ When a word has two consonants (CC) with one vowel (V) on either side of it, the spelling pattern is called the VCCV pattern. This means vowel-consonant-consonant-vowel. To divide these VCCV words into syllables, you usually divide between the two consonants VC/CV. This often means that the first syllable has a short vowel sound.

The **parro**t flew to the top of the w**indo**w.	par / rot	win / dow
He used a m**agne**t to move the l**adde**r.	mag / net	lad / der
Jody wrote a l**ette**r to her s**iste**r.	let / ter	sis / ter
Milton spread the b**utte**r on his toast.	Mil / ton	but / ter

1 Look at the middle part of these VCCV words.
parrot   ladder   letter   butter

What do these four words have in common?

_____

_____

In each group, circle the word that has a double consonant in the middle.
Then write the word and draw a line to divide it into syllables.

2	later	fatter	motor	_____
3	bottom	beach	beaten	_____
4	miser	mist	missing	_____
5	button	brick	bat	_____
6	kennel	kin	kink	_____
7	walk	well	willow	_____
8	spring	summer	sunshine	_____

Name _____

Deep in the Ocean

Look back at the last page and think about what you learned about VCCV words. Then look at the pairs of words in the box.

hop	hopping	swim	swimmer
mad	madder	pit	pitting
rob	robber	fur	furry

When you add a suffix to a one-syllable word that ends with one vowel and one consonant, think carefully. If the suffix begins with a vowel, you sometimes have to double the consonant.

Add the suffix to each word below. Then write the complete word on the line. Divide the new word into syllables.

Word   +   Suffix   Complete Word

1. pat   -ing   _____

2. hit   -er   _____

3. dig   -er   _____

4. shut   -ing   _____

5. fun   -y   _____

6. star   -y   _____

7. Look at the words you have written in numbers 1–6 above. They all have the same spelling pattern. Circle the correct name for the spelling pattern.

   CVCE   CVVE   VCCV   VCV

Fluency: **Reading with Phrasing**

Deep in the Ocean

When actors learn a speech, they learn it in phrases, or groups of related words. Actors, and readers, have to choose when to pause and when to breathe. It is best to say or read a speech or a poem in a way that helps make the meaning clear to your listeners. Practice reading the poem below three times, varying the pace and volume of your voice for effect.

Way,
  way,
    way,
down
deep,
down through the blue,
down through the green,
down through the dark,
down to the bottom,
there is another world.

Deep in the,
dismal,
gloomy,
murky,
depths,
with no sun,
with no moon,
with no stars,
with no light,
hides an eerie world.

Strange,
bizarre,
puzzling,
outlandish,
unheard of creatures,
like angler fish,
like fangtooth fish,
like oarfish,
like black dragon fish,
enjoy happy lives
    in their deep, dark world.

—Robbie Butler

Reading: **Comprehension**

1 Read the word at the top of each box. Find the word in the poem on page 33. Write the words that immediately follow the word on the lines. Write one word on each line.

Verse 1 Way	**Verse 2** Deep in the	**Verse 3** Strange
_____	_____	_____
_____	_____	_____
_____	_____	_____
_____	_____	_____
_____	_____	_____

2 What is the poet trying to make you see with these lists of words?

    Ⓐ Almost any words will do if you use a lot of them.

    Ⓑ The bottom of the ocean is deep, dark, and strange.

    Ⓒ Danger lurks at the bottom of the ocean.

    Ⓓ Nothing can live in the ocean.

3 Read the last line of the poem. It is a surprise. The repetition of the heavy words like *deep, dark, gloomy, murky,* and *outlandish* leads you to expect something sad or scary. You don't expect to hear that life in such a place is happy and enjoyable. What is the main point the poet is making?

    Ⓕ There are lots of strange and unusual fish in the ocean depths.

    Ⓖ Light doesn't shine in the ocean because the sun can't reach it.

    Ⓗ Just because a place is different, doesn't mean it isn't a good place.

    Ⓙ The ocean deep is dangerous, and sad animals live there.

Vocabulary: **Frequently Confused Words**

Deep in the Ocean

★ Some words sound alike but are spelled differently and have different meanings. It is best to learn when to use one rather than the other. When you write, you will have to check carefully to be sure you haven't mixed up these words.

Read each sentence and think about the word choices within the parentheses. Then circle the word that correctly completes each sentence and write it on the line.

1 I'm not allowed in the lake because (its, it's) too deep. _____

2 The whale had seaweed on (its, it's) flippers. _____

3 (Heel, He'll) be here at seven. _____

4 (Wears, Where's) the seal gone? _____

5 (Hears, Here's) the boat. _____

6 Soon (wheel, we'll) go aboard the boat. _____

7 Those are (their, they're, there) lifejackets, not ours. _____

8 If (your, you're) joining us, climb aboard. _____

9 (Theirs, There's) room enough for all of us. _____

10 I think (we've, weave) found a good captain. _____

11 He (lets, let's) us take the boat out in the winter. _____

12 The captain (want, won't) keep the boat out in a storm. _____

13 The harbormaster said (weed, we'd) better come in early. _____

14 The captain said he would (heed, he'd) the warning. _____

15 Do you know (whose, who's) boat that is? _____

Vocabulary: **Content Words**

Deep in the Ocean

⭐ When you read, write, or talk about science and nature topics, certain groups of words are useful. Such words are called *topic-related words* or *content words*. Sometimes these words have other meanings in other contexts. The first sentence in each pair below uses topic-related words to discuss the ocean. The other sentences use those same words in an everyday, or ordinary, context.

Read the following groups of sentences.

The ocean *floor* lies at the bottom of the deepest part of the ocean.
We walked carefully across the slippery *floor*.

The huge *waves* crashed into the rocks.
As the train passes, a little girl *waves* from the window.

We found a *shell* on the beach.
The house had been gutted inside and was little more than a *shell*.

Read each pair of sentences. Which sentence uses the content word in a topic-related context?

---

1 Ⓐ Tiny sea creatures *float* on or near the surface of the water.

　　Ⓑ For the parade we made a huge *float*.

2 Ⓕ I have a *ridge* on my nose.

　　Ⓖ The tops of that mountain *ridge* rise above the water's surface.

3 Ⓐ At the end of the continental *shelf*, the ocean bottom drops sharply away.

　　Ⓑ Please put the book back on the *shelf*.

4 Ⓕ Today our class talked about *current* events.

　　Ⓖ The *current* in this part of the bay is very strong.

5 Ⓐ That picnic basket full of food should *tide* us over until dinner.

　　Ⓑ The *tide* will not go out for at least another hour.

In the Sea

Imagine that you are walking from the shore into the ocean. As you walk out into the water, you find that the bottom of the ocean slopes gently down as you go. This gradual slope from the shore is called the continental shelf.

As you travel farther along the shelf into the ocean, the water gets deeper. At its deepest points, the shelf lies under some 660 feet of ocean water. The continental shelf extends in some places as far out as 100 miles into the ocean. In other places, from other shores, it may only continue about one mile into the water.

At the end of the continental shelf, the ocean bottom drops sharply down, 2 to 5 miles. This steeper slope is called the continental slope. At the bottom of this continental slope, you will find the ocean floor.

From this floor rise mountains, taller than any on land. Deep trenches with steep sides cut into the ocean floor. Some are 7 miles below the ocean surface. Strange life forms live this far down in the ocean.

Advantage Reading Grade 4 © 2004 Creative Teaching Press

If you were walking along the ocean floor, you would see that the underwater mountains look like normal land mountains. The water covers some ocean mountains. Others extend up above the ocean's surface.

Mountain chains called ridges run along the ocean floor. Some of these ridges have tops that stick far above the water. Many of these ridge tops form islands, like Iceland and the Galapagos Islands, of turtle fame. One such island mountain is in Hawaii. Mauna Kea, an old volcano, rises over 5 miles from the ocean floor. Of all the mountains that rise out of the oceans to form islands, Mauna Kea is the tallest.

As well as mountains that rise up, the ocean floor has trenches that drop straight down. These deep cuts have steep sides that go deep into the earth. The deepest one drops nearly seven miles or more below the ocean floor. This is the Mariana Trench in the Pacific Ocean. You can't get much closer to the center of the planet than that.

Reading: **Comprehension**

After reading *In the Sea* on pages 36–37, answer questions 1 through 4.

1 What is the main topic of this nonfiction piece?

     Ⓐ pollution and how it affects ocean creatures

     Ⓑ how the sea benefits people and animals

     Ⓒ the geographical structure of the ocean

     Ⓓ islands, volcanoes, and mountains

2 Which of the following does NOT explain the meaning of the word *gradual*?

     Ⓕ all at once, abruptly, suddenly

     Ⓖ a little at a time, little by little

     Ⓗ slowly, gently, changing by degrees

     Ⓙ bit by bit, step by step

3 Number these three parts of the ocean in the order you would see them if you could walk from land to the ocean's deepest point.

    ____ ocean trench   ____ continental shelf   ____ ocean floor

4 Write two or three sentences that you think would describe what you would see, hear, and feel if you went down to the ocean floor and looked into an ocean trench.

_____

_____

_____

_____

Noting Details
When reading nonfiction, you have to figure out the main idea, but there will also be important facts and details to notice and remember. Paying attention to content words and other topic-related vocabulary will help you understand both the main ideas and the details.

AFRICA

Atlantic Ocean

Ascension Island

Only a Turtle Knows

She knew it was time to go. She didn't know how she knew. She just knew. The other turtles had been slowly streaming down to the water for hours. She was lying sleepily in the sun. Then suddenly, she knew. Like all the other female Atlantic green turtles around her, she knew. It was time to make her way to the island where she was born. She got up, stretched, and lumbered down the beach toward the water.

As she entered the water, she changed. She began to move more quickly. No longer an ungainly, plodding slowpoke, she swam gracefully. She looked around for one last meal. She would leave this lovely feeding spot, here on the coast of Brazil. She would travel over 1,200 miles. The journey would take her several months. There would be no food. She wouldn't eat again until she returned here many months from now.

After her snack, the female turtle really took off. She headed east. She knew the way. She didn't know how she knew the way, but she did. Even if she had been able to talk, she couldn't have explained it. She just sort of felt her way. She sensed magnetic forces that guided her. She used the tides and the ocean currents as "signposts." People use rivers as landmarks. Ocean currents are really just rivers, so they make good "landmarks" for turtles.

Weeks and weeks passed. Still she swam on. She was now hundreds of miles from her home on the Brazilian coast. As she knew she must, she kept swimming without stopping to eat. Her body fat, stored over the long, lazy months on the coast, kept her going. She had just enough energy stored in that body fat to get her to the island and back. She sniffed the water ahead. Then she swam up to the surface for a much-needed breath of air.

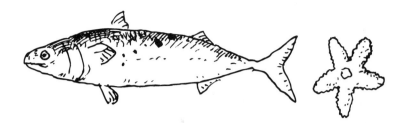 

As do all turtles, she had poor eyesight. Although she couldn't see the sky clearly, there was something about the way the sun, moon, and stars shone down on the water. Something about the way their light filtered down underwater helped point the way. She couldn't really think about it. She just followed all these signs that only the other turtles could understand.

She didn't know it, but she was part of a huge migration. Every two or three years, this migration takes place. Atlantic green turtles, both male and female, set off at roughly the same time of the year. It's not the exact same time of the year, because after all turtles don't have calendars. But they seem to know when it's time to head off to their breeding beaches. The females always go back to the island of their birth to lay their eggs. They swim from the coast of Brazil to Ascension Island in the South Atlantic. But she couldn't think about that. She needed to swim. She had to get to the island before all the good male turtles had been taken. She needed a mate. She needed to lay eggs in the same sand where she had hatched out of her egg all those years ago. That's what this journey, this migration, was about.

After a few months, she knows she's nearly there. Apart from the smell, she has seen other turtles she knows. The sunlight reaches all the way down almost to the ocean bottom. That tells her that she is close to land. Other things tell her that she is close to the right land. She knows. She doesn't know how she knows, but she knows.

Finally, she reaches the shoreline. In the shallows, all the turtles are swimming and looking at each other. She chooses a mate. Later, when it grows dark, she and the other female turtles clamber onto the beach to lay their eggs. They have come to the beach at high tide. They have laid their eggs far enough up the beach that the tide won't wash the eggs away. They have to know how far up the beach the high tide will come. Luckily, as it's already high tide, they can tell which places are safe. And they don't have so far to swim.

She finds a spot and begins to dig. She digs for nearly an hour. Then she rests for a few minutes and digs for a while longer. At last she has made the nest deep enough. She crawls into the hole. She knows it is time to lay her eggs. After almost another hour has passed, she has laid about 100 eggs. She covers them with sand. She is tired and wants to go back into the water to rest. Over the next weeks, she will repeat this nest digging and egg laying every 10 to 14 days. She will leave hundreds of eggs, each group safely buried in a different nest under the warm sand.

It is time for her to go. She will never see her eggs hatch. She will not be there to see the crabs and lizards dig up and eat many of the eggs. She will never see the tiny turtles that hatch out after two months. These baby turtles will fit in the palm of a human hand. Yet tiny creatures will have to fight their way down the beach to the sea. Then they have to throw themselves in the ocean and swim the 1,200 miles back to Brazil to join the adult turtles. They have to do all this with no adults to protect or feed them.

Crabs, fish, and seabirds lay in wait to eat the tiny turtles. Only one or two of every 1,000 baby turtles will survive. The female turtle was lucky. She survived to adulthood. Maybe one or two of her babies will survive, too. But she will never see them. She never saw her mother. She might not know her mother if she did. She doesn't think about this. It is time. She and the other adult turtles will now go back to the feeding grounds near Brazil. She has another 1,200 miles or more to swim before she gets a meal. She's beginning to think about that meal. She knows it's definitely time to go. She doesn't know how she knows, but she knows.

Author's Postscript

Humans do not know how the adult Atlantic green turtles find their way from Brazil to Ascension Island. No one knows how they manage to swim such vast distances without eating or stopping. How the tiny baby turtles manage to swim the same distance shortly after birth is a more baffling question. How do they survive all the dangers waiting to kill them? How do they find their way to a place they've never been to join adult turtles they've never seen? No humans know. Only the turtles know.

Reading: **Comprehension**

After reading *Only a Turtle Knows* on pages 39–41, answer questions 1 through 7.

1 Who is the main character of this story?

    Ⓐ the sea   Ⓒ a male turtle

    Ⓑ an egg   Ⓓ a female turtle

2 Why are the turtles going to swim over 1,000 miles to Ascension Island?

    Ⓕ The island is their breeding ground, where they will lay eggs.

    Ⓖ The island is their feeding ground, and they go every month.

    Ⓗ The turtles go there because the weather is better than Brazil's.

    Ⓙ The turtles leave because of pollution in their feeding grounds.

3 Which is one of the signs that helps the female turtle find her way?

    Ⓐ fish and seals

    Ⓑ boats and airplanes

    Ⓒ sea currents and tides

    Ⓓ her mother and other turtles

4 This story contains lots of facts. How do you know this story is fiction rather than a true story?

    Ⓕ Brazil and Ascension Island are both real places, as is the Atlantic Ocean.

    Ⓖ The author tells what the turtle knows and does not know.

    Ⓗ One of the characters is a fantastic mythical beast that could never exist in the real world.

    Ⓙ It doesn't have a happy ending, and no turtle could swim 1,200 miles without eating.

Fact or Fiction

Fiction stories can contain many facts and true details. In a realistic fiction story, the people seem real and the events are believable. The setting may even be real, as it is in the story you just read. However, if the main character or characters are made up, and the events never really happened, the story is fiction.

                                                    Advantage Reading Grade 4 © 2004 Creative Teaching Press

Reading: **Comprehension**

5 Why is it so amazing that some of the baby turtles manage to swim back to Brazil?

_____

_____

6 Reread the first paragraph of the story. Then read the author's postscript. Why do you think the author called this story *Only a Turtle Knows*?

_____

_____

7 Write at least one fact about each category.

How turtles find their way	How turtles lay eggs	Baby turtles

Know THE Skill

Categorizing
Grouping facts into categories by topic can help you remember important details. It doesn't matter whether the facts appear in a fiction book or a nonfiction book, listing them in some sort of order will help you understand and remember them.

Name _____

Deep in the Ocean

⭐ The kinds of life forms you find in the ocean depend largely on the relative depth of the ocean water. To see how scientists divide the ocean into different zones or depth levels, look at the diagram. Then answer questions 1 through 4.

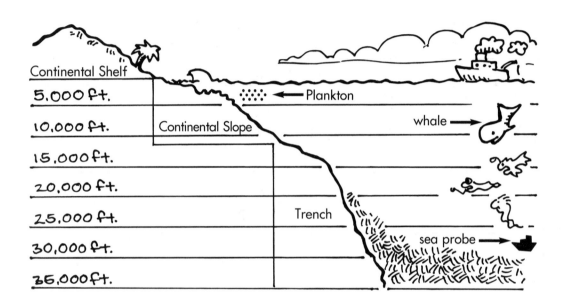

1. Would you be more likely to see plankton in an ocean trench or from the deck of a boat in the middle of the ocean? _____

2. Would you use a sea probe to study whales? Why or why not?

   _____

3. The ocean floor lies at the end of the continental slope. How far down would you have to go to touch it? _____

4. According to this diagram, how deep is the ocean trench? _____

Writing: **Realistic Fiction**

Deep in the Ocean

⭐ When you write a story, you want to get your readers interested. To draw them into your story world, you need to make that world an interesting one. It is important to have a good idea in your own mind of the setting. The setting is when and where the story takes place. Remember that setting means more than just the country, town, or city. Setting can be as specific as in "the closet in the hallway" or as general as "on a planet in another galaxy." Setting also means the time: the century, the day of the week, or the time of day.

On the next page you will write a realistic fiction story. Think about possible plots, characters, and settings. Use the chart below to help you organize your ideas. Write at least two ideas for each story element. Pick one from each category to see if that gives you ideas for a story.

Story Element Planning Chart

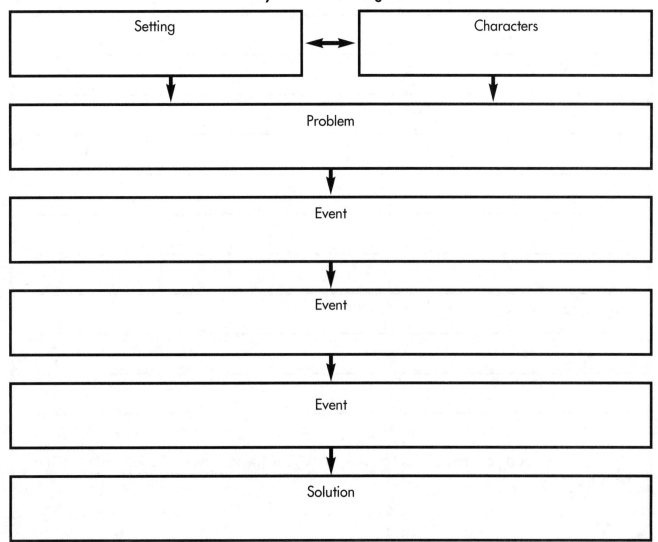

Setting	Characters

Problem

Event

Event

Event

Solution

Write your realistic fiction story on the lines below. Use separate sheets of paper if you need more room.

_____

_____

_____

_____

_____

_____

_____

_____

_____

_____

_____

_____

_____

_____

Have a friend read your realistic fiction story. Ask your friend if he or she learned anything from the story.

Advantage Reading Grade 4 © 2004 Creative Teaching Press

Play with Rhyming Words

Look back at the words listed on pages 27–30. With a friend or parent, see how many rhyming words you can come up with. Then try making up silly rhymes about sea creatures. You might want to read some of Ogden Nash or Edward Lear's poems about animals. You can find them in any library.

Ocean Travels

Do you know who was the first person to design a submarine? Leonardo DaVinci, who died in 1519. Find some books about early methods of sea travel and exploration. What strange methods have men tried to travel underwater? Draw a machine that would let you travel all over under the ocean, even to the deepest depths.

Find Out Where Animals Live

Look at an animal atlas or look on the Internet to find where on earth certain animals live. You'll find that Australia has some rather unusual animals. You'll find other unusual ones at the North and South Poles. Find out about animals that can live in both salt and fresh water. Draw a picture of an ocean habitat that you think your favorite sea animal would like.

Make a Chart

At the library or on the Internet, find out about animal journeys and migrations. Make a chart to show which animals travel the farthest.

Compile Amazing Facts about the Ocean

Collect facts about the ocean, similar to the ones you read on pages 36–37 about how deep the trenches are and how high the mountains underwater can be. Then use your facts to make a quiz game to play with your family or friends.

Check out these books.

Eyewitness: Fish by Steve Parker (DK Publishing)
Eyewitness: Seashore by Steve Parker (DK Publishing)
Eyewitness Juniors: Amazing Fish by Mary Ling (DK Publishing)
The Incredible Journey by Sheila Burnford (Bantam Doubleday Dell)
The Man Whose Mother Was a Pirate by Margaret Mahy (Viking Press)
Oceans by Anna O'Mara (Bridgestone Books/Capstone Press)

Comprehension: Prior Knowledge

In the Movies

Movies are filmed either on a set in a studio or on location. A film set is a place made up to look like somewhere else. Films shot on location can be filmed anywhere in the world. These days, filmmakers use computers to create many parts of a movie. Some movie sets exist only on a computer. There is no set and no location. Think about
• movies you have seen.
• television programs you have watched about how films are made.
• anything you have read or heard about filmmaking.

What would you expect to see if you visited a film set or a film location? Add to the chart some other things that you might find.

People in Front of the Camera	People Off Screen	Filming and Recording Equipment	Other Equipment	Non-Film Essentials
extras (actors with no lines to say)	producer	microphones	lights, props	food, trucks, toilets

Structural Analysis: **Regular Plurals**

In the Movies

⭐ To most nouns, you just add *s* to form the plural. You add *s* to these types of words:
- most singular nouns: *producers, crews.*
- most nouns ending in *o* **IF** the *o* follows a vowel: *videos, rodeos.*
- many nouns ending in *o: pianos, photos.*
- nouns ending in *y* if the *y* follows a vowel: *days, monkeys.*
- some nouns that end in *f* or *fe: roofs, safes.*

Write the plurals of the following nouns.

1 camera _____

2 light _____

3 actor _____

4 truck _____

5 film _____

6 extra _____

To certain types of nouns, you add *es* to form the plural:
- nouns that end in *s, x, z, ch,* or *sh: dresses, foxes, churches.*
- most nouns ending in *o* **IF** the *o* follows a consonant: *potatoes, heroes.*
- nouns ending in *y* if the *y* follows a consonant, but first you change the *y* to *i: puppies, tries.*
- some nouns that end in *f* or *fe,* but first you change the *f* to *v: wolves, hooves.*

Write the plurals of the following nouns.

7 wish _____

8 waltz _____

9 tomato _____

10 city _____

11 thief _____

12 half _____

Name _____

Structural Analysis: **Irregular Plurals**

In the Movies

⭐ Some words have irregular plural forms.

child, children	foot, feet	mouse, mice
man, men	tooth, teeth	ox, oxen
woman, women	medium, media	goose, geese

Some words do not change from singular to plural. You use the same word for both singular and plural meanings.

deer	traffic	corps	trout
sheep	dozen	wheat	salmon
moose	barley	series	bass

Some nouns are used only in the plural. They have no singular noun form.

scissors	trousers	clothes	pants	pliers	slacks

Underline the error in each sentence, if there is one. Then write the correct plural form of the noun on the line at the end of the sentence. If there is no error, write "Correct" on the line.

1. The movie's monster appeared to have only two foots. _____

2. Newspapers and other assorted mediums advertised the movie. _____

3. The carpenter asked the actor to pass the plier. _____

4. Filming stopped when a flock of sheeps ran towards the actors. _____

5. The star ate two trouts for lunch. _____

6. The next scene took place in a field of wheats. _____

7. The wardrobe mistress brings trunks of clothes to the set. _____

Structural Analysis: **Prefixes**

Production Director

In the Movies

A **prefix** is a group of letters that you can add to the beginning of a word to change the meaning. Prefixes have their own meanings, and these usually come from Latin or Greek words. Knowing the meaning and spelling of some common prefixes can help you work out the meanings of many words that you meet as you read.

> *pre-* = "before, earlier than, in advance, or in front of."
>   pre + view = preview
>   "to view in advance, to see beforehand."
>
> *post-* = "after, later, following after or behind"
>   post + game = postgame
>   "after the game"
>
> *non-* = "not, other than, absence of, reverse of, or lacking"
>   non + sense = nonsense
>   "lacking sense or the absence or reverse of sense"

Read the sentences. Choose one of the three prefixes to add to a word from the word list. Use the new words to complete the sentences. Write the new word on the line. The first one is done for you as an example.

Prefixes
non-   pre-
post-

Word List			
flight	binding	script	war
arranged	profit	stick	wrapped

1. The sandwich meat had been ___**prewrapped**___ so she couldn't see how fresh it looked.

2. The charity ran a _____ shop to give clothes to the needy.

3. She added a _____ to the end of her letter because she forgot to tell him the date and time.

4. The director and producer met at a _____ place and time.

5. The actor's agent would not let him sign anything but a _____ contract, one that he could get out of easily.

6. The cook used the _____ pan so he needed only a tiny bit of oil.

Name _____

Production Director

In the Movies

Read the following words. Use one of the prefixes *pre-*, *post-*, or *non-* to make a new word. Write a brief definition of the new word in the space. The first one is done for you as an example. Use a dictionary if you need to.

	Prefix	+ Word	New Word	Definition
1	pre	+ cut	precut	sliced beforehand
2	_____	+ teen	_____	_____
3	_____	+ print	_____	_____
4	_____	+ date	_____	_____
5	_____	+ trial	_____	_____

Read each sentence. As they stand, these sentences don't make sense because there is one wrong word in each. Change the underlined words by adding a prefix that makes the sentence make sense. Write the new word on the line.

6 My sister is allergic to milk so she can only eat <u>dairy</u> ice cream.
_____

7 The coach gave the team members a long <u>game</u> talk about the plays they were supposed to use in tomorrow's championship. _____

8 The store was having a <u>holiday</u> sale on December 23rd and 24th.
_____

9 The buildings built after 1776, therefore after the colonial period ended, are examples of <u>colonial</u> architecture. _____

10 The doctors said there was no need to keep the children away from school and from other children since the disease was <u>contagious</u>. _____

In the Movies

The advertisement below is a casting call. It is sent out to local TV and radio channels to announce local auditions. Pretend you have been asked to read the advertisement over the school loudspeaker as part of the morning announcements. Read the memo aloud. Here are some ways to make your reading smooth and clear:

- Read the ad silently several times to be sure you understand the meaning.
- Be sure that you understand the meaning and pronunciation of each and every word. Ask for help if you don't.
- Underline key phrases such as date, place, and time.
- Make sure you say exactly what is printed.
- Call attention to key points or words by pausing before you say them or by speaking a bit louder.

Here's Your Chance to Be in a Movie!

Kids Picks Films will hold auditions for their next film on Saturday, June 20th.

Supporting Actor Roles
    1 girl, age 10–12, must have five years of ballet.
    1 boy, age 10–14, must have some formal voice training, not just church choir.

Speaking Parts, 5 lines and under
    3 girls, ages 9–11, must have three years of ballet.
    4 boys, ages 10–14, must have three years of ballet.
    6 boys and girls, ages 3–7, with some voice training.

Extras
    25 students for school scenes

Auditions will take place at Westside High School at 9 a.m. on Saturday, June 20th. Bring a parent or guardian to sign legal forms. You will need a birth certificate or passport to prove your age and your most recent report card. Wear comfortable clothes and shoes, suitable for school. Dancers should bring a leotard, tights, ballet slippers, and pointe shoes. Do not wear makeup or costumes. You may have to wait all day to audition, so you should bring a packed lunch, snacks, and bottled water.

Reading: Comprehension

After reading the ad on page 53, answer questions 1 through 4.

1 Who is holding the auditions and advertising them?

    Ⓐ Westside High School   Ⓑ Kids Picks Films

2 Why should you bring food and water?

    Ⓕ The auditions may last all day.   Ⓖ The film crew will be hungry.

How do you know?

_____

3 If you are a 15-year-old boy who has sung in the school chorus for two months, should you go to the audition?

    Ⓐ yes   Ⓑ no

How do you know?

_____

4 What are the most important details to remember from this advertisement? Fill in the graphic organizer with details from the advertisement.

To sign legal forms and prove your age, bring:		Clothes to wear and bring:
_____ _____	When and where will auditions will be held? Date _____ Time _____ Place _____	_____ _____
What not to wear: _____		Also bring: _____

Vocabulary: **Frequently Confused Words**

In the Movies

★ Some words sound alike or almost alike but are spelled differently and have different meanings. These words are called **homophones.** Readers and writers sometimes confuse these words. Watch out for them and learn the differences.

forth, fourth	marry, merry	overdo, overdue
to, too, two	do, due, dew	dye, die

Write the correct words from the list to complete each sentence.

1. The farmer took _____ more rabbits _____ the

   pet shop, but they already had _____ many.

2. Everyone was enjoying a _____ Christmas lunch when John

   announced that he was going to _____ Mary.

3. After the third group failed to return, the _____ group of knights

   marched _____ into the forest.

4. Please don't _____ it when choosing library books to check out.

5. You didn't finish reading the last batch in time and had to pay _____

   fines on two of the books.

6. He likes to _____ his hair in summer.

7. The roses did not _____ until November last year.

8. What do you plan to _____ to save the deer?

9. The hunters are _____ here any minute and they will be able to see

   the deer tracks in the _____ on the lawn.

Vocabulary: **Content Words**

In the Movies

⭐ Many English words have more than one meaning. This is often true of content words. Content words often have one meaning in ordinary daily life contexts. But they can take on a different meaning in certain situations.

Read each sentence. Then choose a word from the box. Write the word that makes sense in the sentence. You will use each word more than once.

1 The _____ keeps the insects out of the room.

The computer _____ is dark.

2 Just point the _____ and click to open the computer file.

The _____ ran across the floor to get the cheese.

3 Look at the _____ and choose what you want to eat.

Open the _____ and choose CLOSE before you turn off the computer.

4 Find middle C on the piano _____ before you begin to play.

To turn off the computer, first press the key on the _____.

5 The archeologists found an ancient _____ buried in the temple ruins.

_____ down the list until you find the right application.

6 You can have many computer _____ open at the same time.

Please close the bedroom _____ as it is too cold.

7 Plug the printer plug into the printer _____ at the back of the computer's base.

San Francisco is still a _____ city with many ships loading and unloading their cargo at the docks there.

mouse
windows
port
keyboard
scroll
screen
file
crash
menu

How to Make a Movie

Making a movie normally involves many people doing different jobs. A movie is almost always a team effort. Making a movie can take months or years. People who make movies, large or small, go through these steps.

The Idea

Movies begin with an idea. Writers turn this idea into a script or screenplay. Sometimes the script comes from an original idea. Sometimes writers adapt the script from an existing book or play.

Producers and Directors

The producer is in charge of the movie. He or she has to raise money to pay for the project. The producer normally chooses the director. The producer and director will work for months or even years before actors and crew turn up to shoot the first scene. Eventually, the director will hire a crew. The director will decide which actors to cast. Often, a storyboard artist will draw each scene of the movie so that everyone can see the script as a series of pictures. Everything will be carefully planned.

Sets, Locations, Props, and Costumes

A production designer creates the setting for the film. He or she will do research to find or build the right setting for that one film. The production designer will choose locations and design sets. He or she will also oversee props and costumes. They must fit the setting's place and time.

Makeup

Actors, and their stunt doubles, have to look the part. They must look the same throughout a scene, even if it takes weeks to shoot. Complex makeup can take four or five hours. The makeup has to be put on fresh every day—and must look exactly the same as the day before.

Shooting the Film

Before filming, the producer, director, and their team will schedule and plan the film in great detail. All the props, sets, costumes, stunts, and effects will be ready in advance. The actors will have rehearsed for weeks. When everyone is ready, only then does the whole group gather. The director decides which shot to begin with. Then filming starts. Scenes are rarely shot start to finish in script order. The last scene may be shot first.

Editing

After filming ends, the director and the editors cut huge chunks of the film. They piece together the shots they think work best. An editor can make a movie look completely different from the one the actors and crew thought they shot. The sound track and the film are synchronized together at this stage. What results is the film you see at the movies.

Reading: **Comprehension**

After reading *How to Make a Movie* on pages 57–58, answer questions 1 through 5.

1 What is the purpose of the first paragraph?

    Ⓐ It explains what the production designer will do.

    Ⓑ It tells about the importance of makeup.

    Ⓒ It introduces the steps involved in moviemaking.

    Ⓓ It connects movies to television.

2 What do you think the word *synchronized* means in the following sentence from the passage?

    "The sound track and the film are synchronized together at this stage."

_____

3 Which of the following happens first in the moviemaking process?

    Ⓐ The director rehearses the actors.

    Ⓑ The storyboard is created.

    Ⓒ The editor cuts large chunks of film.

    Ⓓ The makeup artist gets the star ready for filming.

4 Which of the jobs described in *How to Make a Movie* would you MOST like to do? Why?

_____

_____

_____

5 Which of the jobs described in *How to Make a Movie* would you LEAST like to do? Why?

_____

_____

Know the Skill

Sequence
When you are reading or writing nonfiction, like instructions or directions, sequence is very important. Readers must know exactly which step comes first, second, next, and so on until the final step. Look for key direction words such as *first, next, then,* and *finally* to help you keep track of sequence.

Colleen had a dog named Asta. Her great-grandmother, whom she called Grandma Doris, gave her the puppy for her seventh birthday. That was three years ago. Now she was ten, and Asta was three. Colleen had never liked the dog's name. Her great-grandmother named Asta before she gave him to Colleen. Colleen's mother and grandmother, Grandma Grace, would not let her change the name. They said it was a special name. One day Colleen would understand why.

One Saturday morning, Colleen and her mom had just eaten breakfast with her Great-Grandma Doris and her Grandma Grace. The two shared a big house in Hancock Park in Los Angeles, near Hollywood. Both ladies were widows. Both had dogs just like Asta. Grandma's dog was named Nick. Great-grandma's dog was Nora. On the mantle were photos of Colleen's great-grandfather and also of her grandfather. In the pictures were other dogs that looked like Asta. One had been named Charles. In one picture, her wedding photo, Grandma Doris looked very young, younger than Colleen's mom. So did her great-grandfather. In that wedding picture, there was a dog named Asta and a puppy named Astatoo. As she always did, Colleen asked Grandma Doris to talk about the dogs.

"As you know, dear, Nick here is your Asta's father. Nora is Nick's mother. So she is your Asta's grand-mother. Charles, the dog in that picture with your grandpa, is your Asta's great-grandfather. Astatoo is his great-great-grandfather. And Asta was his great-great-great-grandfather," said Grandma Doris.

"So Asta is really Asta number three. Why didn't you call him Asta-three? That's how you named Astatoo, isn't it?" asked Colleen.

"Of course it is," said Grandma, "but you can spell well enough to know that Astatoo contains a play on the words *two* and *too*. We didn't think Asta-three had the same ring. Also, since there is no other Asta alive in the family now, there was no reason not to name this one plain Asta."

After breakfast, Grandma Doris and Grandma Grace told Colleen to put the leashes on the three dogs. Then the four generations of women and the three generations of dogs set out for a walk. They walked just a few streets away to a French restaurant that Colleen knew well. It had a nice terrace outside. Both grandmas had taken Colleen there many times. Like real French restaurants in France, this one allowed dogs, so the family liked to go there. But today something different was going on.

There was a film crew shooting there. The director and the producer turned to look at the women and the dogs. Colleen thought to herself, "They'll make us leave. I'd have liked to watch them film."

"Ladies, you're here at last! We're so glad to see you. All of you," smiled the director as she bent over to shake hands with Nick, Nora, and Asta.

The producer gave each dog a dog biscuit. Suddenly, another dog appeared. It looked just like Nick, Nora, and Asta. All four dogs wagged their tails. They seemed happy to see each other. A very large man walked over to the dogs.

"Myrna, I see you've found your brother. Hello, young lady. Meet Myrna," said the large man as he pointed to the fourth dog. "Myrna will be starring in this picture. She is allowing me to co-star. I am Henry. You must be Colleen. Your grandmother has told me all about you and Asta. Did you know that I used to work with both your Grandma Grace and your Grandma Doris? I'm almost part of the family. Myrna is part of the family."

Grandma Grace explained that Myrna and Asta were from the same litter. They were indeed brother and sister.

"But how did you work together? I know you used to train dogs, but what did Henry do?" Colleen looked from Grandma Doris to Grandma Grace.

Henry laughed loudly. "Did you not know that your great-grandmother and then your grandmother after her were famous? They trained all the best animal stars in Hollywood. For 50 years the small screen and the large screen showed animals trained by your dear grandmammas."

"You never said . . . You mean you worked in the movies?" Colleen was so surprised she could hardly speak.

"We did tell you. We used to talk about the dogs and cats and other animals all the time," reminded Grandma Grace.

"Yes, but you never said it was for the movies! You used to say you trained this bird for Mr. Hitchcock or this horse for Mr. Wyler or this dog for the thin man. You never talked about movies!" wailed Colleen.

"I guess we never did make it clear that Hitchcock and Wyler were famous Hollywood directors. And *The Thin Man* referred to a whole series of movies that ran from 1934 to 1944 and after became a TV series," explained Grandma Doris.

"*The Thin Man* movies had three stars—William Powell, Myrna Loy, and Asta, their dog. Now who do you think Asta belonged to? And what do you think we're filming here today? We're making a sequel called *The Not-So-Thin Man,* starring Myrna and me." Henry's eyes twinkled at Colleen.

Just then, a loud crash came from inside the restaurant. Myrna came bounding out onto the terrace covered in something pink. She was tracking it everywhere.

The director and producer came racing out behind the pink dog. Colleen picked Myrna up, only to discover that the pink was contagious. Suddenly, her shirt turned pink, as did her arms and hands. The director explained that the set design people were using a big sink in the kitchen to dye some tablecloths pink. Myrna had jumped into the sink.

"What will we do? We have to shoot Myrna's main scene today. That pink dye won't wash off for weeks!" The producer was almost in tears.

Grandma Doris reached down and picked up Asta. "Don't worry. We brought along a stunt double. You'll find that Asta is even better trained than Myrna. And since the script has the actors calling the dog Asta, no one will be confused. Here's your new star. He'll be just as good as his great-great-great-grandfather."

"Grandma, do you mean that Asta in your wedding picture is the Asta that starred in *The Thin Man* movies? Asta was a real movie star! Now I know why you didn't want me to change his name." Colleen's eyes grew wider and wider.

"And now there will be one more star in the family. Your Asta will be the sixth generation to play in the movies. This is a much bigger surprise than we planned. Asta will be a real star dog," said Grandma Doris.

When Asta heard his name, he stood on his hind legs and barked three times. Perhaps he was saying, "Lights! Camera! Action!"

Reading: **Comprehension**

After reading *Star Dog* on pages 60–62, answer questions 1 through 4.

1 Why doesn't Myrna get to star in the film?

    Ⓐ Her fur has turned pink from the dye in the sink.

    Ⓑ She is in trouble for barking too much.

    Ⓒ The director wants a dog related to the real Asta.

    Ⓓ Henry doesn't want to co-star and doesn't like Myrna.

2 This story mentions real places, real actors, real directors, and real movies. How do you know it is a fictional story and not a true one?

    Ⓕ The dogs would not be movie stars in real movies.

    Ⓖ The names of the characters and the dogs are too odd.

    Ⓗ The introduction said that it was fiction and imaginary.

    Ⓙ The restaurant allows dogs inside and that can't be true.

3 What did Colleen's grandmother and great-grandmother do in the movies?

_____

_____

4 Explain the important cause and effect upon which the plot depends. In other words, what is the main event that causes the story to turn out as it does?

_____

_____

_____

_____

Cause and Effect
Every story has a plot, and in every plot certain events cause other events to happen. To understand plot, you need to look for causes and their effects. Something happens to a character because something caused it to happen. Effects are the results of causes.

Name _____

In the Movies

Graphic Information: Tables

⭐ You may not realize it, but you read tables all the time. Every time you look at a TV schedule in the paper or in a television guide, you are reading a table. When you look up the movie listings to see what's playing at your local mall or movie theater, you are reading a table.

Study the movie schedule. Then answer questions 1 through 5.

What's Playing This Weekend

Clay Classic Cinema

Gone with the Tide, uncut
2:00, 6:00, 10:00
15-minute intermission

Multiplex at the Mall

The Case of the Missing Script
1:00, 3:15, 5:30, 7:45, 10:00

101 Spotted Dogs and Striped Cats
11:30, 1:00, 2:30, 4:00, 5:30
family discount for children under five

In a Galaxy Not Too Far Away
1:00, 3:00, 5:00, 7:00, 9:00

Central Casting Movie House

In a Galaxy Not Too Far Away
12:15, 2:15, 4:15, 6:15, 8:15, 10:15

1 What time does the last showing of the mystery film begin? _____

2 Which movie is obviously for children? How do you know?

_____

3 How long is *Gone with the Tide,* not counting the intermission?

_____

4 You can't get to the movie theater before 3 and you have to be home by 6. Which movie can you NOT see?

_____

5 Which movie is playing at two theaters?

_____

Name _____

Production
Director

In the Movies

Writing: **Reviews**

⭐ When you are writing to compare two things, you have to point out for your readers the ways in which the two things are alike and different. You compare their similarities and contrast their differences.

Think of two movies you know well or have seen recently. How were they alike? How were they different? What were the similarities and differences in plot, character, and setting?

Write a review of the two movies explaining their similarities and differences. To get started, complete the Venn diagram below.

movie _____   movie _____

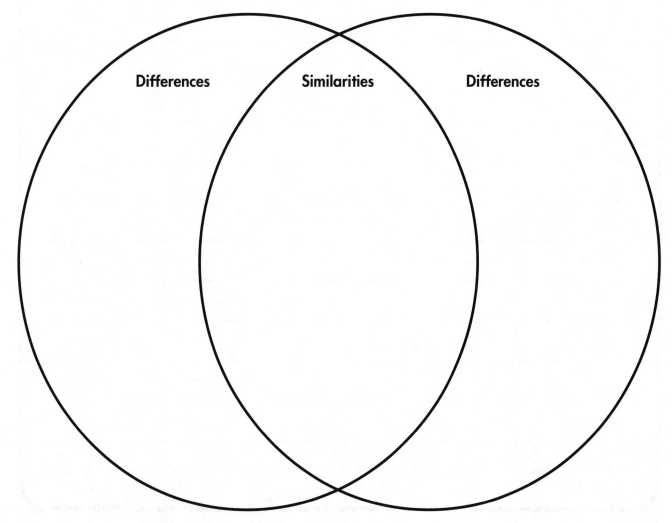

Differences   Similarities   **Differences**

Write your review on the lines below. Use a separate sheet of paper if you need more room.

_____

_____

_____

_____

_____

_____

_____

_____

_____

_____

_____

_____

_____

_____

Have a friend read your review. Ask your friend which movie he or she would most like to see.

Learn about Moviemaking

Did you know that the Indian film industry, often called Bollywood, makes more films and more money off films than Hollywood does? What is the most expensive film ever made? Look at books, magazines, and Internet sites about the film industry and moviemaking to see how many interesting facts you can find. Make a chart that tells about the steps involved in making a movie. Draw a picture or a symbol for each step, then write a caption for each.

Keep a Film Diary

Write a summary of each film that you see over the next month or two. Write what you liked about each film and what you didn't like.

Make a Chart

At the library or on the Internet, find out which directors made your favorite movies or which actors starred in your favorite movies. Make a table or chart showing all the films your favorites have made. Look at film encyclopedias and film dictionaries for ideas.

Write a Poem

Try writing a speech or poem of your own about movies or plays. To get inspired, read aloud these lines from William Shakespeare's play *As You Like It:*
"All the world's a stage,
And all the men and women merely players;
They have their exits and their entrances;
And one man in his time plays many parts."

Write a Script

Use the story *Star Dog* as the basis for a Reader's Theater script. You can write it out with speaking parts for yourself and your friends or family members, then you can perform it. Use a narrator to fill in the parts that don't work as speeches.

Check out these books.

Eyewitness Film by Richard Platt (Knopf Publishers)
Eyewitness Science: Light by David Burnie (DK Publishing)
Eyewitness Science: Technology by Roger Francis Bridgman (DK Publishing)
If You Take a Mouse to the Movies by Laura Numeroff and Felicia Bond (HarperCollins)
Lights, Camera, Action: Making Movies from the Inside Out by Lisa O'Brien (Owl Communications)
Special Effects by Jake Hamilton (DK Publishing)
That's a Wrap: How Movies Are Made by Ned Dowd, David Mamet, et al. (Simon & Schuster)

A Ride on the Train

Comprehension: **Prior Knowledge**

Transportation has changed greatly in the last 100 years. Today, we can travel to the other side of the world in only a day. But for 200 years, one machine has been the mainstay of public travel—trains. We use trains for long journeys and for short journeys. Trains carry people, goods, and animals.

What do you already know about trains? Add to the web some other things that you know or might expect to learn about trains.

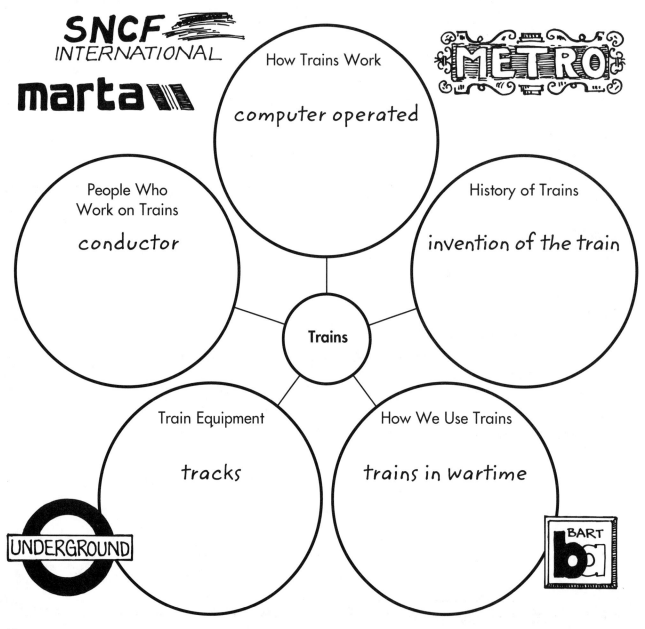

SNCF INTERNATIONAL

marta

How Trains Work

computer operated

METRO

People Who Work on Trains

conductor

History of Trains

invention of the train

Trains

Train Equipment

tracks

How We Use Trains

trains in wartime

UNDERGROUND

BART

Structural Analysis: Suffixes for Words Ending in -y

A Ride on the Train

★ A **suffix** is a letter or group of letters that you add to the end of a word to change the meaning and the way you use it.

Rules for Spelling Words with Suffixes

- The spelling of the suffix itself never changes.
- The spelling of the word to which you are adding the suffix sometimes does change.
- If the word ends in a vowel followed by -y, just add the suffix: *enjoy, enjoys, enjoying, enjoyed.*
- If the word ends in a consonant followed by -y, change the *y* to *i* and then add the suffix—as long as the suffix does not begin with *i: beauty, beauties.*
- If the word ends in a consonant followed by -y AND the suffix begins with *i*, then keep the *y* so you don't have two *i*'s together: *study, studying.*
- Watch out for one-syllable words that end in -y. You usually keep the *y*, except when adding -*es* or -*ed*, in which case you change the *y* to *i: dry, drying, dryer* but *dries* and *dried.*

Add the suffixes and write the new words on the lines. If there is no such word, write an X in the space. The first one is done as an example.

	Base Word	Add -s or -es	Add -ing	Add -ed	Add -er
1	marry	marries	marrying	married	X
2	obey				
3	worry				
4	copy				
5	fry				
6	delay				
7	employ				
8	supply				
9	cry				

Name _____

Structural Analysis: Suffixes for Words Ending in -e

A Ride on the Train

★ Think twice when adding suffixes to words that end in -e. When you add a suffix to a word that ends in silent e, look at the word and the suffix. Remember the following rules.

Rules for Adding Suffixes to Words Ending in -e

- If the suffix begins with a consonant, keep the final e at the end of the word: *nine + -ty = ninety*
- If the suffix begins with a vowel, drop the final e on the word: *hope + -ing = hoping*; *simple + -y = simply* (note that in a suffix the letter y acts as a vowel)
- If the suffix is *-able* or *-ous* and the word ends in *-ge* or *-ce*, you often keep the e. You do this to keep the consonant sound soft: *notice + -able = noticeable*; *outrage + -ous = outrageous*
- If the suffix begins with a vowel AND the word ends in *-ye*, *-oe*, or *-ee*, keep the final e: *dye + -ing = dyeing*; *hoe + -ing = hoeing*; *agree + -able = agreeable*
- If the word ends in *-ie*, you change the *ie* to y before adding the suffix *-ing*: *die + -ing = dying*
- Sometimes, you can choose whether to keep or drop the final -e since both spellings are correct: *lovable or loveable*

Join the word and the suffix. Write the new word on the line.

1. damage + -ing = _____

2. store + -ed = _____

3. compete + -ing = _____

4. like + -able = _____

5. cute + -est = _____

6. courage + -ous = _____

7. tie + -ing = _____

8. eye + -ed = _____

Advantage Reading Grade 4 © 2004 Creative Teaching Press

Name _____

A Ride on the Train

Structural Analysis: Suffixes -ar, -er, and -or

⭐ The suffixes *-ar, -er,* and *-or* often mean "one who" or "that which."
Here are some examples:
• lie + -ar = liar, meaning "one who lies"
• teach + -er = teacher, meaning "one who teaches"
• sting + -er = stinger, meaning "that which stings"

Read the sentences. Choose one of the three suffixes to add to a word from the word list. Use the new words to complete the sentences. Write the new word on the line.

Suffixes			**Word List**				
-ar	-er	-or	beg	visit	drive	profess	survive
			stick	clean	post	audit	conduct

① Since there is a fast train into town, I am a frequent _____ to the city.

② I take the bus to the station at least once a week, so the _____ now recognizes me.

③ Last month, my friends and I helped the station _____ pick up trash on the station platform.

④ We picked up litter and helped him scrape off a large _____ that someone had stuck on the glass case that displays the timetable.

⑤ As she checked our tickets on the train, the _____ thanked us for helping clean the platform.

⑥ She is very nice and used to be a _____ at a famous university before she moved to this country.

⑦ Sometimes when I'm in the city I visit my great-grandmother's friend who is a _____ of the Titanic disaster.

⑧ She was an accountant and until she was 85 she was still the official _____ for several big companies.

⑨ My friends and I like to walk around the city, but we usually do shop for at least one book, CD, or _____ at the bookshops and music stores.

Name _____

Word Building: **Suffixes**

A Ride on the Train

Read the following words. Add suffixes to make at least one new word for each of the 20 words. Then use the suffixes and words to make as many more new words as you can. Follow the rules you learned in the previous three lessons. Use a dictionary if you need to.

Words

heavy	sad	invest	appear
buy	unite	visit	perform
key	care	govern	act
pry	complete	invent	noise
hurry	damage	joy	disagree

Suffixes

-or	-ly	-less	-s
-er	-ous	-ful	-tion
-ar	-ness	-ed	-ion
-y	-ance	-ing	-ment

_____ _____ _____ _____

_____ _____ _____ _____

_____ _____ _____ _____

_____ _____ _____ _____

_____ _____ _____ _____

_____ _____ _____ _____

_____ _____ _____ _____

_____ _____ _____ _____

_____ _____ _____ _____

Advantage Reading Grade 4 © 2004 Creative Teaching Press

A Ride on the Train

Fluency: Reading with Accuracy

⭐ Pretend you are a railroad employee assigned to read announcements over the loudspeaker. It is important that you read each announcement clearly, quickly, and accurately. Here are some ways to make your reading smooth and clear:

- Read the announcement silently several times until you understand the meaning.
- Be sure that you understand the pronunciation of every word.
- Underline any word or phrase that you think you may get wrong.
- Make sure you say exactly what is printed.
- Make sure you speak clearly and distinctly so everyone, especially travelers whose English is not fluent, will understand what you say.

When you can read the announcement without making any mistakes, ask an adult to listen to you read it.

Bookstack Station, Your Attention Please!

Now boarding on Platform 2: the After School Special train to Bookville. This train will depart at 4:15. This is 15 minutes later than scheduled. Therefore, arrival times will be 15 minutes later than scheduled. We expect to reach Bookville at 6 p.m. We apologize for this delay. Our steam engine driver has a cold. We had to wait for another driver to heat the water to make steam.

The train will stop at the following stations:
- Pooh Corner
- Treasure Island
- Wonderland
- Never Never Land
- Hobbit City
- Pottertown Central
- Bookville

Passengers for Earthsea, Narnia, and Camelot, please change trains at Treasure Island.

Please have your tickets ready to show the conductor. For security reasons, please keep your luggage with you at all times. Please turn off all cell phones and CD players. Books, of course, are allowed.

Reading: **Comprehension**

After reading the announcement on page 73, answer questions 1 through 6.

1 The train is leaving later than scheduled. What time was it scheduled to leave?
In other words, what time should it have departed?

    Ⓐ 4 o'clock   Ⓒ 4:15 p.m.

    Ⓑ 6 o'clock   Ⓓ midnight

2 Why should you keep your luggage with you at all times?

    Ⓕ to prevent anyone from tripping over it

    Ⓖ so no one takes it by mistake

    Ⓗ for security reasons

    Ⓙ in case you forget it and leave it behind

3 Can you make and receive calls on your cell phone once the train is moving?
How do you know?

_____

4 If you are going to Camelot, do you stay on the train until it stops in Bookville
at 6 o'clock? Why?

_____

5 Pretend you are going to Never Never Land. Which stop is it, and what is the stop
before it?

    Ⓐ the last stop, Pottertown Central

    Ⓑ the first stop, there is no other stop before it

    Ⓒ the fifth stop, Hobbit City

    Ⓓ the fourth stop, Wonderland

6 What must you have ready when you board the train? Why?

_____

Advantage Reading Grade 4 © 2004 Creative Teaching Press

Name _____

A Ride on the Train

⭐ Some words sound alike or almost alike but are spelled differently and have different meanings. These words are called **homophones.** Readers and writers sometimes confuse these words. Watch out for them and learn the differences.

> right—suitable, appropriate
> write—to form characters or symbols on a surface
>
> stake—a pointed piece of wood
> steak—a slice of meat

Next to each word below, write another word that sounds like it but has a different spelling and a different meaning. Read the clue to help you.

1	rows	_____	a flower
2	cheep	_____	not expensive
3	urn	_____	to receive by doing hard work
4	foul	_____	a chicken is one
5	fir	_____	animal covering
6	tow	_____	at the end of your foot
7	crews	_____	travel by boat
8	grown	_____	a noise
9	maze	_____	a type of corn
10	slay	_____	a type of sled
11	sore	_____	to fly high
12	sun	_____	male offspring

Name _____

A Ride on the Train

⭐ Transportation is an important part of life for all of us. We travel somewhere almost daily, even if only to school and back. Whether we walk, ride in a car, or take a bus, subway, train, boat, or plane, we need to know and use certain words.

Think of words related to different types of transportation. In each of the boxes below, list words related to the topic.

Car	
door	_____
gas	_____
highway	_____
traffic lights	_____

Bus	
fare	_____
seats	_____
driver	_____
stops	_____

Subway	
underground	_____
car	_____
carriage	_____
token	_____

Train	
engine	_____
locomotive	_____
tracks	_____
station	_____

Plane	
airport	_____
wings	_____
pilot	_____
arrivals	_____

Boat	
dock	_____
deck	_____
captain	_____
cabin	_____

Read the poem. Listen to the rhythm and the beat.
Then answer the questions on pages 78–79.

Train Trip

by Robbie Butler and Matt White

This is the train leaving the station
for a long trip across the nation.
Picking up speed as she passes the river,
with people and goods and mail to deliver.

With train cars old and train cars new,
a shiny engine whose metal gleams blue.
Pulls them along uphill and down
through wheat fields and corn fields and deserts burnt brown.

The train carries timber, cattle, and stone,
families with children, people alone.
Round mountains she climbs, through valleys she streaks,
scaring birds in the trees when her shrill whistle shrieks.

Passing the signal, her speed starts to drop.
The train must slow quickly to make the next stop.
As she pulls to the station, the passengers wait.
They look at the clock. They won't be late.

Doors of the carriages slide open wide
to let people off then more pile inside.
Darkness can't stop her, so throughout the night,
she races the stars, plays tag with moonlight.

Though she thunders past barns, not one cow awakes,
but the bank windows rattle and the church steeple shakes.
With sunrise behind her, she crosses the West.
When she reaches the sea, only then does she rest.

Reading: **Comprehension**

After reading the poem on page 77, answer questions 1 through 10.

1 Read the lines from the poem silently, then read them aloud. The poets wrote the poem to sound a certain way when read aloud. What does the beat and rhythm of the poem sound like?

    Ⓐ the wind blowing through the trees

    Ⓑ the shrill whistle of a train

    Ⓒ the birds flapping out of the trees

    Ⓓ a fast train chugging along

2 The poem talks about the train as if the train were a person. What pronouns do the poets use to refer to the train?

    Ⓕ she, her   Ⓗ it, its

    Ⓖ he, him   Ⓙ I, mine

3 Explain how you can figure out that the train is heading west from the lines in the poem.

_____

_____

4 Circle the word that does NOT rhyme with these words: *streaks, shrieks*.

    peaks   weeks   breaks

5 Circle the word that does NOT rhyme with these words: *down, brown*.

    grown   clown   frown

6 Circle the word that does NOT rhyme with these words: *night, moonlight*.

    fright   lit   write

7 Circle the word that does NOT rhyme with these words: *river, deliver*.

    driver   quiver   shiver

 Advantage Reading Grade 4 © 2004 Creative Teaching Press

Reading: Comprehension

8 If you were making a documentary or travel film about a train, which scenes from the poem would you show? Choose two lines from the poem and describe what you would show on screen to go with these two lines.

_____

_____

_____

_____

9 Draw a sketch, like a storyboard, to show what the viewer would see in the scene you described in number 8 above.

10 Think about what happens in the poem "Train Trip." Think about the scenes it describes and the information it gives. Now retell the poem in another way. You can turn it into a rap, a song, or a story or a piece of nonfiction writing. Write your draft on a separate sheet of paper.

This is a nonfiction article about the history of railroads. Read the article carefully.
Then answer the questions on page 83.

A Short History of Railroads

Who built the very first railroad or railway? No one knows. The ancient Greeks cut grooves into stone blocks. Then they placed the stones in lines. They could guide wheeled carts along these lines. You can still find remains of these stones all over Greece. Long before, earlier peoples used the same idea. They knew it was easier to direct a wheel if you could guide it along.

In the 1500s, people wrote about early attempts to make "railed roads." There is a German book, dated 1516, about mining. Its drawings show a truck with four wheels that rolled on wooden rails. In 16th and 17th century Britain*, people used early "wagon-ways" with wooden rails. These rails guided small wagons along a short way. Horses had to pull or men had to push these wagons.

These wooden-railed "roads" were only a few hundred yards long. They carried goods to and from mines and quarries**. Later, they were used to carry coal, stone, and iron ore to the nearest river. People still relied on boats to carry goods for longer distances.

*Britain – once called Great Britain, the United Kingdom includes England, Scotland, northern Ireland, and Wales

**quarry – a place where people dig materials out of the ground, usually stone, slate, or limestone for building

These wagon-ways sloped down to the river. Full wagons rolled down the hill. The goods were loaded onto boats. Horses pulled empty wagons back uphill on the rails. At Wollaton, England, one of these wagon-ways was built from 1603 to 1604. This is known as the first railway in Britain.

From the 1600s to the 1700s, coal and iron ore use grew. So the use of wagon-ways spread. In the 1700s and early 1900s, other industries also used these wagon-ways. But these wagon-ways were private. They didn't go far. So the public could not use them.

In 1803, the first public wagon-way opened. It was in the south of England. The Surrey Iron Railway still carried goods only. But anyone could pay to send goods on this wagon-way. In 1807 in Wales, the first passenger wagon-way opened. It was a world first. People could pay money and ride on a railway! This railway still relied on horses to pull the wagons.

A new invention brought changes. The steam engine could power a locomotive*. In Britain between 1802 and 1803, Richard Trevithick built one. He built the first steam locomotive to run on rails. They were wooden wagon-way rails.

Others invented stronger locomotives. But wooden rails were weak. So the early steam locomotives had few uses. Better tracks soon made steam trains more useful. At last, railway came to mean what it does today.

In 1825 in northern England, a new steam railway opened. It carried both freight and people. This was a first! In 1830, a second one opened. From then, steam trains spread throughout the world. By 1900, rail networks covered the U.S. and Canada. They also spread across Europe and parts of Russia.

*locomotive – a self-propelled vehicle that runs on rails

Reading: Comprehension

After reading the article on pages 80–82, answer question 1 through 5.

1 Who were the first people to use lines cut in stones to guide wheeled carts?

Ⓐ modern Greeks

Ⓑ people who lived long before the ancient Greeks

Ⓒ the British in the 18ᵗʰ and 19ᵗʰ centuries

Ⓓ Americans in the 20ᵗʰ century

2 Why is the drawing in the German book about mining important to the history of railroads?

Ⓕ It shows the first picture of a modern steam train, though it was never built.

Ⓖ It copied the ancient Greek ideas and used stones for rails.

Ⓗ It proves that by 1516 the idea for railed wagon-ways was well-known.

Ⓙ It was drawn by a famous German painter and is an example of her work.

3 What powered the carts that rolled on the wooden wagon-ways from the 1500s until 1804?

_____

_____

4 Why did wooden rails limit the use of the first steam locomotives?

Ⓕ They all ran in circles and didn't go far.

Ⓖ Timber was scarce and people couldn't build many rails.

Ⓗ The steam made the wooden rails bend and melt.

Ⓙ The wooden rails were not strong enough.

5 The modern system of rail networks came about because of two events in the history of railroads. What were these two events, that marked a turning point in the history of railroads?

Ⓐ the invention of the steam engine and improved tracks

Ⓑ quarries and mines that were too far from rivers

Ⓒ troops and supplies for the two world wars

Ⓓ airplanes and cameras so people could map the rail routes

Name _____

Graphic Information: **Maps**

A Ride on the Train

⭐ Not all maps show oceans, rivers, continents, and countries. Some don't show streets or roads. When you travel on a rapid transit or subway train, you will see on the wall a map that shows all the stops and stations. These maps depict the subway route and stops in a special way to make it easier to understand.

Book City Subway Trains

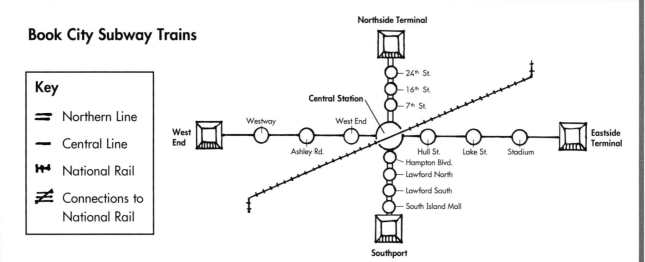

Key

⇒ Northern Line

— Central Line

⋈ National Rail

⇄ Connections to National Rail

1 You live on the north side of town, just a few blocks from the 24ᵗʰ Street subway station. You want to go to the city's only shopping mall. Which line would you take?

   Ⓐ Central Line   Ⓒ National Rail line

   Ⓑ Northern Line   Ⓓ all of the above

2 You live on the north side of town, just a few blocks from the 24ᵗʰ Street subway station. You are taking the subway to a National Rail Station. At which station do you get off to catch the train?

   Ⓕ Northern Terminal   Ⓗ Eastside Terminal

   Ⓖ Southport   Ⓙ Central Station

3 You live on the north side of town, just a few blocks from the 24ᵗʰ Street subway station. Your two best friends live near Ashley Road Station. How many stops must they PASS after they get on the train at Ashley Road Station BEFORE they get off at 24ᵗʰ Street Station to visit you?

   Ⓐ 2   Ⓒ 6

   Ⓑ 4   Ⓓ 8

Advantage Reading Grade 4 © 2004 Creative Teaching Press

Name _____

A Ride on the Train

Writing: **Directions**

⭐ When giving directions, you must be sure you tell each direction in the right order. You must be sure to give exact information. If you leave something important out, people could get lost. You need to think about important landmarks that will let people know they are on the right road. You have to tell them when to turn left or right. You must also give exact street addresses.

Choose two places in your neighborhood that you know very well. Make sure they are not too far apart. Complete the chart below. Use the information from the chart to write directions telling a reader how to get from one place to another. Write the directions on page 86.

	Place 1: Start and Finish	Place 2: Start and Finish
Street Addresses		
Landmarks You Pass on the Way		
Right Turns and Left Turns		
Road Signs or Traffic Lights		

Now write step-by-step directions so that a reader could use your directions to walk from one place to another. Remember to put the directions in the correct order.

_____

_____

_____

_____

_____

_____

_____

_____

_____

_____

_____

_____

_____

_____

Have a friend read your directions. Ask your friend if he or she understands how to get to the location.

Learn about Trains

What else would you like to know about trains? Look at books, magazines, and Internet sites about trains and railroads to see what else you can find out. Make a list of the people whose inventions moved rail travel forward.

Keep a Train Diary

Make notes about every train you ride on or see. Some people, called train spotters, travel all over just to get a sight of one train or engine to add to their list of trains they've spotted.

Make a Scrapbook

You can find many pictures of trains in magazines and travel brochures. You'll also find lots on the Internet. Search the Internet for information about trains, railroad history, and railway museums. Some of the steam train locomotives from the early 20th century looked really special. You can also find posters of some of these really beautiful machines. Visit the British National Railway Museum Web site for more about early trains: www.nrm.org.uk.

Collect Poems and Songs about Trains

Many poets have written about trains and train journeys. There are also many songs about train travel, particularly folk songs. You can also look for songs and poems about Casey Jones, a steam train driver, and John Henry, a folk hero who worked on the railroads.

Make a Dictionary

Start a list of words related to trains, locomotives, and railroads. You'll find you know some of them already. Have you ever heard of a cowcatcher? Look it up in a dictionary to find out what it means.

Check out these books.

Across America on an Emigrant Train by Jim Murphy (Clarion Books)
Big Book of Trains by Christine Heap (DK Publishing)
John Henry by Julius Lester (Puffin)
The Railway Children by E. Nesbit (Puffin)
Train to Somewhere by Eve Bunting
  (Houghton Mifflin)

Name _____

At the Pool

Comprehension: **Prior Knowledge**

What is your idea of the perfect swimming pool? Would it have a slide? A fountain? A wave machine? Would it have underwater caves and ruined castles, like a large fishbowl? On the lines below, write a short description of your paradise pool. Then draw a picture to show how it might look.

_____

_____

_____

_____

_____

_____

Name _____

At the Pool

Structural Analysis: **Silent Letters**

 We often spell words that contain silent letters. When you say the word *should*, you do not hear the *l*. The *l* is silent.

These letters are the letters that are most often silent.
They tend to be silent when certain other letters are with them.

- silent *b*—after *m* and before *t*
- silent *g*—before *n* or *h*
- silent *h*—at the beginning of some words and sometimes after the letter *w* or *r*
- silent *k*—before *n*
- silent *l*—before *d, m,* or *k*
- silent *n*—after *m*
- silent *p*—always before *s, n,* or *t*
- silent *w*—before *r*

Say each word. Circle the silent letter. Write the silent letter on the line next to the word. Then write the entire word in the second space. This will help you remember its spelling.

1. plumber ____ _____
2. debt ____ _____
3. gnaw ____ _____
4. sign ____ _____
5. hour ____ _____
6. rhyme ____ _____
7. knit ____ _____

8. could ____ _____
9. half ____ _____
10. yolk ____ _____
11. column ____ _____
12. know ____ _____
13. whole ____ _____
14. wrong ____ _____

Name _____

At the Pool

Each of the following words is missing one or two silent letters. Read the clue. Add the missing silent letter(s) to complete the word. Write the correctly spelled word in the space.

1 _host   _____   a costume you see at Halloween

2 han_some   _____   good-looking or attractive

3 thou_ _t   _____   past tense of *think*

4 cu_board   _____   old Mother Hubbard's was bare

5 b_ild   _____   to make or construct

6 _terodactyl   _____   a dinosaur

7 dau_ _ ter   _____   the opposite of *son*

8 r_inoceros   _____   an animal that looks like an armored tank

9 su_tle   _____   not obvious

10 i_land   _____   surrounded by water

11 lis_en   _____   what you do to hear a soft sound

12 depo_   _____   a building for railroad or bus users

13 ans_er   _____   the opposite of *question*

14 ya_ _t   _____   a very large, luxury boat

15 s_ience   _____   a school subject, often taught in a lab

16 shou_d   _____   rhymes with *wood*

Structural Analysis: Synonyms and Antonyms

At the Pool

★ **Synonyms** are words that mean almost the same thing. One example is *laugh* and *giggle*. An **antonym** is a word of opposite meaning. The word *up* is the antonym (opposite) of the word *down,* and vice versa.

Complete the following list. For each numbered word, supply the missing synonym or antonym by writing it in the space.

	Word	Synonym	Antonym
1	shout		whisper
2	blunt	dull	
3	capture		release
4	laugh	giggle	
5	part	portion	
6	hot	baking	
7	discover		lose
8	difficult		easy

9 Choose a word from the synonym list and write a sentence using it.

_____

_____

10 Choose a word from the anotnym list and write a sentence using it.

_____

_____

Structural Analysis: Word Building

At the Pool

In the first box, you will find mixed-up pairs of words. Some pairs are synonyms. Some are antonyms. Sort them out. On the lines labeled *Synonyms*, write the pairs of words that mean the same or almost the same. On the lines labeled *Antonyms*, write the pairs of words that mean the opposite of each other.

Mixed-Up Word Pairs

right	fancy	enemy	present
sell	anger	fetch	amaze
friend	surprise	gift	buy
bring	plain	wrong	rage

Synonyms

_____   _____

_____   _____

_____   _____

_____   _____

Antonyms

_____   _____

_____   _____

_____   _____

_____   _____

Advantage Reading Grade 4 © 2004 Creative Teaching Press

Name _____

At the Pool

⭐ Whenever you read a script for a play or Reader's Theater, the "actors" must read the parts with expression, so it sounds real. Also, each character's voice must sound different. Otherwise, listeners will get confused. Practice reading the script below and change each character's voice. Use expression to make it sound like real people are talking.

Ice Cream Heroes

Narrator	On a hot July day, Cal and Jenny took their two dogs, Dan and Daisy, to Laurel Lake to swim. They went with their Aunt Louise and her two-year-old, Tony, their baby cousin.
Jenny	What luck Aunt Louise wanted to come. Mom would never have let us come alone.
Cal	Uh, oh. Tony has an ice cream cone and two new best friends. Look, he's giving Dan a lick of the ice cream. Next is Daisy's lick, now Tony's. Who says kids don't know how to share?
Jenny	Aunt Louise is on the case. Tony won't have any skin left when Aunt Lou finishes scrubbing the dog germs off his face. Here they come.
Cal	Aunt Lou, we'll take Tony in the lake and wash the ice cream off him. He's got his inner tube. Come on pal, let's go.
Narrator	Cal and Jenny lead Tony out into the lake, where he happily floats between them, giggling and splashing in his inner tube. Suddenly, a speedboat zooms into the swimming area, making huge waves.
Cal	Hey! Can't he see there are little kids swimming here?
Jenny	Cal! Help! Oh, no! Tony slipped out of the inner tube! He's floating away. He's way over there—face down.
Narrator	Cal and Jenny both swim as fast as they can. The wash from the speedboat has rapidly carried Tony far away. They won't reach the toddler in time. But two unofficial lifeguards are on duty.
Cal	Good dogs. Good dogs. You saved him, thank goodness.
Jenny	Thank goodness Dan and Daisy are golden retrievers and know how to pull small creatures from the water without hurting them. Tony's giggling again so he must be OK.
Narrator	Yes, you heard right. Dan and Daisy raced into the lake, swam out, and grabbed Tony. Daisy pulled his arm with her mouth, and Dan lifted him by the seat of his swimming trunks, which were well padded by the diaper underneath.
Cal	I guess it's a good thing Tony shared his ice cream. Dan and Daisy won't let anything happen to their ice cream friend. What heroes!

Name _____

Reading: **Comprehension**

Answer questions 1 through 5 after reading the script on page 93.

1 Who is Tony? Which character tells the audience who Tony is?

_____

_____

2 How do the dogs get to lick the ice cream cone? Who tells about the dogs licking the ice cream?

_____

_____

3 Why do Cal and Jenny take Tony into the lake? Who explains why Cal and Jenny take Tony into the lake?

_____

_____

4 What causes the big waves that carry Tony away? Who explains what causes the big waves and the wash that carries Tony away?

_____

_____

5 Who saves Tony? Who tells the audience how Tony was saved?

_____

_____

Point of View
In every piece of writing, there is a point of view. In this script, we get the story from three points of view. We get both Cal and Jenny's point of view because we hear what they say and we know what they see and do. We get extra information from the narrator's point of view.

Advantage Reading Grade 4 © 2004 Creative Teaching Press

Name _____

At the Pool

Vocabulary: **Frequently Confused Words**

⭐ Some words sound similar but are spelled differently and have different meanings. Some words sound alike and have similar or related meanings.

weather	whether	disprove	disapprove
accept	except	affect	effect
emigrate	immigrate	rise	raise
beside	besides	expect	suspect

Read the definitions. Write words from the box above on the lines to complete each sentence.

1 *Rise* means to get up or go up. *Raise* means to move something up, to increase something, or to grow something.

The farmers _____ many types of potatoes in our region.

2 The verb *affect* means to influence. The noun *effect* means the result of a cause. The verb *effect* means to bring about or cause to happen.

The new boss announced that he was going to _____ some changes.

3 *Weather* means the state of the atmosphere as in rainy, sunny, cold, dry, stormy, etc. *Whether* is an indirect question usually used with the word *or*.

I can't decide _____ to walk or ride my bike.

4 If you show something to be false, you *disprove* it. If you withhold approval and do not approve of something, then you *disapprove* of it.

My sister _____ of my taste in music.

5 If you *accept* something, you agree or you agree to take it. *Except* means leaving out or excluding.

I have done all of my homework _____ the math problems.

Vocabulary: **Content Words**

At the Pool

 Most of us know many weather-related words. Meteorologists are professionals who study the weather. The information they give the public about normal daily weather involves the following words, among many others.

wind speed	temperature	air current	sleet
air pressure	cloud	degree	barometer
wind direction	Celsius	condensation	humidity
hours of sunshine	evaporation	frost	drought
thermometer	Fahrenheit	fog	inches of rainfall
rain	snow	hail	thunderstorm

Sort the words from the list into the following categories. Some words may fit in more than one. If you are unsure of a word's meaning, consult a dictionary, or look in a science book or a nonfiction book about weather.

Measuring and Recording Weather	Types of Weather Conditions	Natural Processes That Affect or Cause the Weather
barometer	cloud	condensation

HOME WEATHER WATCH

What is weather? Weather is the short-term state of the atmosphere. Weather reports describe atmospheric conditions. These relate to heat or cold, wetness or dryness. We also describe these conditions as clear or cloudy, calm or stormy.

Meteorologists measure and record the weather to identify patterns. These weather patterns help them forecast the weather. We use these forecasts to plan our daily lives. Weather forecasts help farmers look after their crops and animals. They help ships avoid danger. Are you planning a pool party? The weather forecasts can help you choose a day when rain is unlikely. The weather affects all of us.

Modern weather forecasting relies on constant observation and measurement. What is being measured and observed? Atmospheric conditions. These are all recorded at the same time worldwide. Meteorologists gather millions of these measurements.

This data* comes from many sources. There are weather stations across the globe. Some sit on small islands far from towns. Others are in the world's busiest cities. Ships collect readings. Weather buoys at sea send data by radio signals. So do weather balloons in the sky. Special high-flying airplanes take readings. From space, weather satellites beam back data. All of this data goes into special computers. Meteorologists use the analyzed data to forecast the weather for the next 24 hours and the next week.

A home weather watch doesn't need fancy tools. You could set up your own weather station with simple tools. You must take measurements once or twice every day at exactly the same time. If you keep records over a long period, they will be more accurate.

You should measure temperatures and rainfall. You should also measure wind speed and direction. Use a barometer to measure air pressure. You should also write down how much of the sky is cloud covered. Soon you will be able to use your own forecast to plan your pool party.

*data – factual information used for calculating and reasoning

Reading: **Comprehension**

After reading the *Home Weather Watch* on page 97, answer questions 1 through 5.

1 What do meteorologists do?

　　Ⓐ study the weather　　　　Ⓒ watch for meteorites

　　Ⓑ travel on boats　　　　　Ⓓ scan the night sky

2 Which of the following pairs of antonyms are NOT words that describe atmospheric conditions?

　　Ⓕ hot, cold　　　　　　　Ⓗ near, far

　　Ⓖ cloudy, clear　　　　　Ⓙ calm, stormy

3 Based on what you know, which of the following would you use to measure wind direction? The answer to this question does not appear in the text. However, the text does tell the purpose of one of the measuring devices below.

　　Ⓐ thermometer　　　　　Ⓒ ruler

　　Ⓑ barometer　　　　　　Ⓓ weather vane

4 How do you think weather patterns help farmers and sailors?

_____

5 In what other jobs or activities might weather forecasts be helpful?

_____

_____

Know the Skill ☞

Extending Meaning

When reading, you need to make connections between what you read and your own life. This often means you have to read between the lines and make inferences. You have to think about how you could use the information you read. In the last paragraph of *Home Weather Watch*, the writer explains what you would measure in a home weather station. She says you use a barometer to measure air pressure, but she doesn't tell you what you use to measure temperature because she assumes you already know how to use a thermometer.

This is a fictional story that takes place in a swimming pool. Read the story carefully.
Then answer the questions on pages 102–103.

Time Divers

Richard loved to swim. He swam almost every day. He dreamed of being on the high school swim team. But he had only just started middle school, so he had a few years to prepare. His favorite swimming pool was near his family's apartment, in the city center. The Glenville Public Bath and Pool House had opened in 1890. The city council had spent millions to build the grandest public baths in the state. They wanted to show how successful the town had become. They wanted people to know what a good place it was to live. They also wanted the thousands of people who did not have indoor plumbing to keep clean and bathe more often. In addition to the big pool, there was a separate baby pool in another room. On the second floor were steam rooms, shower rooms, and some old bathtubs, no longer used.

In winter, the pool was often crowded. But in summer, most people chose to swim in one of the city's outdoor pools. If he came just after lunch, Richard usually had the pool to himself. Only Flo, the friendly elderly lady in the front hall ticket booth, was around in the afternoon. He often saw her going into the pool as he left.

As always, he went to stall 36 to change. The changing stalls stood up against the wall on the right-hand side of the pool. They were fancy cast iron stalls, painted hundreds of times over the years. Now they were a dark blue. But where the paint had chipped, Richard could see that they had once been black. Before that they had been gray. The chips showed that when they were new, they were a deep green, to match the beautiful wall tiles. The baths had not been well kept. Some of the stained glass windows were broken, and many tiles were gone or chipped. As he often did, Richard thought about how cool it must have looked in the old days.

He came out of the stall and walked to the edge of the pool. As always, he admired the mosaic tiles on the floor around the pool. The tiles showed fish, seahorses, and seashells. The same mosaic tiles lined the floor of the pool itself. But those tiles showed even greater skill. Bigger seashells, mermaids, sea turtles, dolphins, and whales decorated the pool floor.

He dove into the clear water. He swam almost the length of the pool. Lungs bursting, he came up for air. He shook his head and wiped the water from his eyes. He couldn't believe what he saw and heard.

The pool was no longer empty. Two girls and a boy splashed in the water at the

other end of the pool. "How did they get here?" he wondered. "There was no one here when I dove in."

He began to swim his usual 100 laps. After 50, he looked up to check his time on the digital clock on the wall. It wasn't there. In its place was a clock with hands. "Oh, well," he thought. "At least it has a second hand so I can check my times. The other one must be broken. They must have stuck this one up until it's fixed."

Then he noticed that the three kids had climbed out and were sitting on the side of the pool. All three had the same bright red hair and deep green eyes. They had to be brother and sisters. The youngest girl looked about his age. Her older brother and sister were busy talking, but the youngest kept sneaking shy glances at Richard. All three had on the strangest swimming gear. The two girls' tops looked like really old-fashioned sailor suits. The bottoms looked like, well, bloomers! Not that Richard had ever seen any except in books. And their brother wore a tank top over what looked like cycling shorts, but they were striped dark gray.

"You're a really good swimmer," the brother said and smiled at Richard. "Are you timing yourself? If so, that clock is off by about 10 seconds."

"That's good news. I thought I was slipping. Thanks for telling me." Richard started another lap. As he did, he heard the older sister say, "Florence, we can only swim for five minutes more." Then he heard splashes as the three jumped into the pool.

He decided to get out and get his stopwatch. He wanted to time himself down to the second. As he walked over to stall 36, he saw that three stalls were filled with the other swimmers' clothes. Their street clothes looked as odd as their swimwear. As he pulled his watch from his bag, he dropped it on the floor. He bent to pick it up, and saw a stack of newspapers, neatly folded. The date on the newspaper was the right day, August 14. But the year said 1895. How could a 200-year-old newspaper look like new? He took his watch and went back to the pool. He laid the watch on the side and dove in again. He swam a few more laps. The three redheads had left the pool and were in the stalls dressing. He thought again about the newspaper. "Must be one of those copies you order from the newspaper. Get the paper that came out on this day in history." He swam a few more laps.

When he stopped to check his time, Richard saw Florence and the other two leaving. The brother turned and waved, then said, "Florence, did you remember your books?"

Their street clothes were weird, too. They looked like something out of a history movie. Then he noticed it. The changing stalls were a deep dark green. He stared and shook his head. He looked up and down the row of stalls. Every one was green—not blue, not black, but green. He took a deep breath and swam down into the bottom of the pool. As he swam, he looked at the tiles. He couldn't find a single missing tile. None were cracked. They looked like new.

He came up for air and climbed out of the pool. As he picked up his watch, he saw a missing tile on the poolside. Then another, and a few feet away he saw others. He looked up at the clock. This was too creepy. The digital clock was

back. He spun round to look at the stalls. Every single stall was blue. The stalls were the same color they had been when he came in to change to swim. He sat down on the poolside and looked down into the water. Even from where he sat, he could see chipped and missing tiles.

Richard dressed quickly and went out to the entrance hall. As he walked up to the counter where Flo the ticket seller sat, he remembered that Flo was short for Florence. He noticed for the first time that the elderly woman who sold him tickets every day had deep green eyes. She looked up, smiled, and said, "All done for today?"

"Yes, all done. By the way, Flo, the three kids who came out a minute ago, who are they?"

"What kids? I didn't see them. What did they look like?" Flo asked.

"Two girls and a boy. They all had red hair and green eyes. The youngest girl was about my age," Richard paused, and thought before he spoke. "They wore really funny clothes."

"What kind of clothes?" Flo leaned forward and stared intently at Richard.

"Well, their swimming clothes and their street clothes looked like something out of history. The girls wore what looked like sailor suits and shower caps to swim. And one of them wore shoes that buttoned." Richard expected Flo to tell him he was crazy.

Instead, she stared at him. Then she smiled and reached for a book under the counter. She pulled out a folded, yellow newspaper page and showed it to him.

"That's them. That's definitely them." Richard felt relieved for a second. Then he saw the date on the newspaper. The date was August 14, 1895.

"I know how you feel," she said. "I've seen them before, several times. Always on this day of the year. Read the article," she handed it to Richard, who read it as fast as he could.

The article was about the three Clarke children. Each had won the city swimming meet for their age group. David Clarke, Sally Clarke, and Florence Clarke. Then he looked at the nametag Flo always wore when she sat behind the ticket counter. It said "Flo Clarke."

"Yes, I'm related to them," said Flo. "David was my grandfather. I was named after my great-aunt, the Florence you see in the old newspaper and the Florence you saw today. And yes, I know it's not possible, but I've been seeing them since I was just a little older than you. I've seen them six times, about once every ten years. It's one of the reasons I keep working here and keep swimming. I only ever see them in the pool. Everyone thinks I swim to stay healthy, and I do. But mainly I swim in hopes that I'll see them again. I was waiting for you to leave so I could get in the pool, since today's the day."

"How? Why? I don't understand." Richard's words and thoughts didn't match up.

"Neither do I. I just think there's something special about this old pool. Every time I dive in, I wonder what will happen. I call it 'diving.' I don't know how else to explain it, and I don't guess I ever will. Will I see you tomorrow, Time Diver?"

Richard nodded. "You bet. And you'll see me next year on this date, too."

Reading: **Comprehension**

After reading *Time Divers* on pages 99–101, answer questions 1 through 10.

1 Who is the main character in this story?

Ⓐ elderly Flo Clarke

Ⓒ Richard the swimmer

Ⓑ young Florence Clarke

Ⓓ David Clarke

2 From whose point of view is the story told? Through whose eyes do we see the story? Whose thoughts do we know?

Ⓕ elderly Flo Clarke

Ⓗ Richard the swimmer

Ⓖ young Florence Clarke

Ⓙ David Clarke

3 How is elderly Flo Clarke related to David Clarke?

Ⓐ David Clarke was her grandfather.

Ⓑ David Clarke was her brother.

Ⓒ David Clarke was her childhood friend.

Ⓓ David Clarke was on her swim team.

4 What color are the changing stalls when Richard first arrives and goes in to change into his swimming gear?

Ⓕ black

Ⓗ gray

Ⓖ dark blue

Ⓙ deep green

5 What color are the changing stalls when Richard is watching the three Clarke kids leave?

Ⓐ black

Ⓒ gray

Ⓑ dark blue

Ⓓ green

6 When Richard goes into the pool building and when he leaves the pool building, we are in the 21st century. In what century did the three Clarke children win their swimming meets and in what century was the Glenville Public Bath and Pool House built?

Ⓕ 21st

Ⓗ 19th

Ⓖ 20th

Ⓙ 14th

Reading: **Comprehension**

7 What is the date on the newspaper that Richard sees next to the boots on the floor of the changing stall?

    Ⓐ August 14, 1995   Ⓒ August 14, 1795

    Ⓑ August 14, 1895   Ⓓ August 14, 2095

8 When Richard first goes in the pool, some of the tiles in and around the pool are missing or chipped because they are 200 years old. What happens to the tiles while the Clarke children are present in the pool?

    Ⓕ The tiles are like new, with none missing or chipped.

    Ⓖ The tiles disappear, as do the changing stalls.

    Ⓗ The tiles change colors, and go from blue to green.

    Ⓙ The tiles move around.

9 What is strange about the clothes the three red-haired swimmers wear?

_____

_____

10 How does Richard explain the clock and the newspaper?

_____

_____

Draw Conclusions
Sometimes fantasy stories start out in the real world. It isn't until the author gives you enough hints or clues that you figure out you are in a fantasy world. Many fantasy stories involve time travel. In time travel fantasy stories, the author has to let you know that you and the main characters have somehow traveled into another time.

Name _____

Graphic Information: **Bar Graphs**

At the Pool

★ Often it is easier to present information in the form of charts or graphs. Graphs are a good way to compare scores. The reader can see at a glance how different scores measure up. Graphs also help you record information in a useful way when you are doing research for science or other purposes.

Study the graph. Then answer questions 1 through 4.

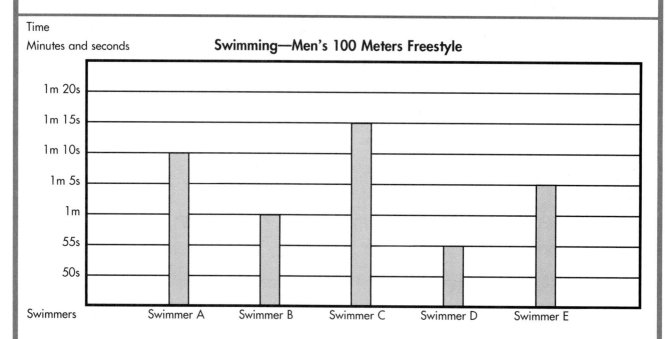

Time
Minutes and seconds

Swimming—Men's 100 Meters Freestyle

1m 20s
1m 15s
1m 10s
1m 5s
1m
55s
50s

Swimmers   Swimmer A   Swimmer B   Swimmer C   Swimmer D   Swimmer E

1 Which swimmer won the meet? _____

2 Which swimmer had the slowest time? _____

3 By how many seconds did the winner beat the swimmer who came in second place?

    Ⓐ 5 seconds   Ⓒ 15 seconds

    Ⓑ 10 seconds   Ⓓ 50 seconds

4 How many seconds does Swimmer C need to cut from his time in order to tie with Swimmer E?

    Ⓕ 5 seconds   Ⓗ 15 seconds

    Ⓖ 10 seconds   Ⓙ 50 seconds

Writing: **Newspaper Account**

At the Pool

⭐ When you read or hear news stories, they usually answer certain key questions in the first sentence or two. These questions are *who, what, when, where,* and *how.* Writers call the first paragraph in an article the *lead paragraph.* You lead with the key information so the reader has all the important facts.

On the next page, write a newspaper article about an imaginary race.

Think about different races you have seen. They can be track events, car races, horse races, swimming races, or snail races. They may be ones you have seen on TV. You can also make up a race and write whatever you want about it. Make a list of races. Circle the idea you will write about. Then, use the chart below to help you decide what to write and to make sure you answer all the key questions in your lead paragraph.

Races I Could Write About

1 _____   **3** _____

2 _____   **4** _____

	Main Points	Other Details	Things to Add in Later Paragraphs
Who?			
What?			
When?			
Where?			
How?			

Decide which race your newspaper article will cover. Then use the chart from the previous page to plan and write your article.

_____

_____

_____

_____

_____

_____

_____

_____

_____

_____

_____

_____

_____

_____

_____

Have a friend read your article. Ask your friend if he or she can answer *who, what, when, where,* and *how.*

Word Practice

Make an antonyms game. Use the lists on pages 91 and 92 to make cards that have antonym pairs on the front and back. You will need at least 10–20 cards with a word on each side. With friends or family, play the game. Draw a card but look only at the top side. The other players will see the back of the card. You read aloud the word on your side. Then you have to give an antonym. The other players will tell you if you got it right or wrong. If you are right, you keep the card. The game ends when all the cards are gone. The player with the most cards wins.

Word Practice

Play "synonym racing." Again using the lists on pages 91 and 92, write words on slips of paper and put them in a hat or box. You will need at least 10 slips. Each player will need paper and pencil. You will also need an egg timer or an alarm clock. With two or more players, draw a word from the hat. See who can come up with the most synonyms for that word before the one-minute time limit runs out. When the time runs out, compare your lists. Settle any disagreements with a dictionary.

Find Pool Records

At the library or on the Internet, find books that contain world records. Record books, almanacs, and top 10 or top 100 books often have lists for the largest swimming pool, fastest swimmer, Olympic records, etc. Some even have short biographies of the record holders. Make your own World Record book about something that interests you. You might even want to design and draw a poster to announce some of the most interesting records you find.

Write a Poem

Look in the library or on the Internet to find poems about swimming. Decide which ones you like best. Then try writing one of your own. Remember, poems don't have to rhyme.

Check out these books.

Breathing Not Required by Michele Martin Bossley (Lorimer)

Get Set! Swim! by Jeannine Atkins (Lee and Low Books)

(Male Sports Stars Series) *Superstars of Men's Swimming and Diving* by Paula Edelson and Howard Keiser (Chelsea House Publishers)

Tom's Midnight Garden by Philippa Pearce (HarperCollins)

ANSWER KEY

Page 5
Answers will vary, but make sure that students place their home state under the correct region.

Page 6
The following 7 answers can be in any order:
1. shell
2. summer
3. apple
4. head
5. rock
6. spring
7. box

The following 7 answers can be in any order:
8. cake
9. by
10. bleed
11. nose
12. kind
13. oat
14. tube

Page 7
1. cupcake; answers will vary. Possible answers include: pale, name.
2. mailbox; answers will vary. Possible answers include: drain, aid.
3. payoff; answers will vary. Possible answers include: tray, today.
4. neighborhood or neighborhood; answers will vary. Possible answers include: weigh, freight.
5. teacup; answers will vary. Possible answers include: pea, least.
6. sweetheart; answers will vary. Possible answers include: green, peel.
7. campfire; answers will vary. Possible answers include: dime, bite.
8. diehard; answers will vary. Possible answers include: spies, pie.
9. highchair; answers will vary. Possible answers include: night, thigh.
10. butterfly; answers will vary. Possible answers include: try, cycle.
11. toenail; answers will vary. Possible answers include: hoe, doe.
12. rainbow; answers will vary. Possible answers include: flow, know.
13. billfold; answers will vary. Possible answers include: poll, bolt.
14. sailboat; answers will vary. Possible answers include: loan, toad.
15. undertone; answers will vary. Possible answers include: robe, home.
16. overrun; answers will vary. Possible answers include: odor, also, go.
17. fruitcake; answers will vary. Possible answers include: cruise, suitcase.
18. flashcube; answers will vary. Possible answers include: tune, ruler.

Page 8
Answers will vary. These answers are possible answers.
1. brain
2. trail
3. day
4. date
5. eater
6. maybe
7. least
8. free
9. cease
10. my
11. light
12. kind
13. fried
14. note
15. toast
16. motion
17. show
18. blue
19. moon

Page 9
1. <u>Groups</u> of states make <u>up the five</u> (regions) of the (United) States.
2. The states in a (region) share (similar features,) such as (landforms,) (climate,) (resources,) and (vegetation.)
3. Georgia, <u>New</u> York, Ohio, California, <u>Maine</u>, West Virginia
4. Texas, <u>New</u> Hampshire, <u>Rhode</u> Island, <u>North</u> Dakota, <u>South</u> Carolina

Page 10
1. milk/shake
2. play/ground
3. foot/ball
4. ham/burg/er
5. (mar/ket)
6. teen/age
7. (chip/munk)
8. (le/gal)
9. night/gown
10. bath/robe
11. (im/press)
12. o/ver/throw

Page 12
1. Here is one possible answer: *You should choose to visit coastal Georgia in winter for a number of different reasons.*
2. Here is one possible answer: *The author wants to convince readers to visit coastal Georgia in winter.*
3. Good weather, outdoor sports, historic sites, and food.
4. Here is one possible answer: *The weather is usually sunny. There are many sports, like golf, tennis, horse riding, and walking on the beach. There are many historic sites and good food.*

Page 13
5. Answers will vary. Here are two possible answers: *I am convinced that I would like to visit coastal Georgia to see Savannah and the historic houses. I would not want to visit coastal Georgia in winter because I like snow.*

Page 13
1. their, there
2. there, they're
3. there's, theirs
4. through, threw
5. through, thorough
6. you're, your
7. your
8. you're
9. there

Page 14
1. left, at
2. at, near, south
3. in, middle
4. inside
5. below
6. above
7. beyond, southeast
8. alongside

Page 16
1. B
2. F
3. The Sioux: moved <u>around</u> or <u>moved from place to place</u>, lived in <u>tipis made from buffalo hides</u>. The Miami lived in the <u>forest</u>, made <u>canoes</u> and fished.

Page 20–21
1. A remuda is a herd of extra horses.
2. J
3. A
4. G
5. Cookie has to get the chuck wagon to the next stop in time to have lunch ready when the cowboys and herd arrive.
6. Answers will vary. Possible answers include: *Because he misses good food and being clean. Because he loves peach ice cream and pecan pie, and he hates being dirty and dusty.*
7. C
8. J
9. Answers will vary, but should include some combination of the following: horses, animals, his sister, Kit, the cook Cookie, pecan pie, peach ice cream, baths.
10. Here is one possible answer: *No, because Jason is the first-person narrator, the "I," the person writing the letter, so only he talks.*
11. Answers will vary but should draw some evidence from the text. Here is

one possible answer: *I like that he loves his sister, that he cares about animals, and that he hates being dirty. I would not like to drink his coffee.*

Page 22
1 the Spanish missions
2 Native Americans
3 because they arrived in 1849
4 from 1822 to 1848, so 26 years

Pages 23–24
Students should write the name of the region or place they will write about and give some ideas about how they will introduce their arguments and fill out the table. The persuasive argument should contain at least two reasons with at least one supporting fact or example for each reason.

Page 26
Answers will vary. Here are some of the possible answers: **The shore:** seaweed, scallop shells, crabs, rocks. **Shallow water:** jellyfish, plankton, small fish, seals, porpoises, rocks, trash from humans. **Deep water:** whales, sharks, rays, tuna, dolphins, shipwrecks. **Deepest, darkest ocean floor:** underwater mountains, volcanoes, trenches, angler fish, viper fish, hatchet fish, rabbit fish, black dragon fish, creatures that don't need light.

Page 27
Answers will vary. Possible **r family blends** include: bridge, cross, drive, friend, growl, pretty, treasure. Possible **l family blends** include: blow, cloak, fling, gleam, plot, slow. Possible **s family blends** include: scar, skin, smooth, snake, sport, stop, sweet. Possible 3-letter blends include: scream, scheme, three, shriek, squirm, sprinkle, splendid, stroke.

Page 28
1 sk
2 sc
3 sp
4 st
5 bl
6 cl
7 fl
8 gl
9 pl
10 sl
11 br
12 cr
13 dr
14 fr
15 gr
16 pr
17 tr
18 tw

Page 29
1 Answers will vary. Possible answers include: bang, sang, rang, gang, tang, slang.
2 Answers will vary. Possible answers include: finger, clinger, ringer, stringer.
3 Answers will vary. Possible answers include: beck, fleck, neck, peck, wreck, trek.
4 Answers will vary. Possible answers include: knocker, mocker, rocker, soccer.
5 Answers will vary. Possible answers include: bunk, skunk, chunk, dunk, junk.
6 Answers will vary. Possible answers include: blinking, drinking, thinking, linking, pinking, sinking.
7 clasp
8 stink
9 strong
10 clock
11 brisk
12 twist

Page 30
1 They all have a double consonant in the middle; in other words, the same consonant appears twice in a row in the middle of each word.
2 fat/ter
3 bot/tom
4 mis/sing
5 but/ton
6 ken/nel
7 wil/low
8 sum/mer

Page 31
1 pat/ting
2 hit/ter
3 dig/ger
4 shut/ting
5 fun/ny
4 star/ry
7 VCCV

Page 33
1 Verse 1
   way
   way
   down
   deep
   down

   Verse 2
   dismal
   gloomy
   murky
   depths
   with

   Verse 3
   bizarre
   puzzling

outlandish
unheard
of

2 B
3 H

Page 34
1 it's
2 its
3 He'll
4 Where's
5 Here's
6 we'll
7 their
8 you're
9 There's
10 we've
11 lets
12 won't
13 we'd
14 heed
15 whose

Page 35
1 A
2 G
3 A
4 G
5 B

Page 38
1 C
2 F
3 3 ocean trench, 1 continental shelf, 2 ocean floor
4 Answers will vary. Here is one possible answer: *As I reached the ocean floor, I felt afraid and excited. The cold was the first thing that struck me. There was nothing to see except blackness.*

Page 42–43
1 D
2 F
3 C
4 G
5 Answers will vary. Here is one possible answer: *The author tells how many other animals are waiting to eat the eggs and then the newly hatched turtles. Then they have to learn to swim soon after they're born. They have to find their way across over 1,200 miles of ocean, and they have to find food and feed themselves.*
6 Answers will vary but should mention that humans have been unable to discover how the Atlantic green turtles accomplish these amazing feats of navigation and endurance. So the author is emphasizing that the turtles know a lot that we don't.

7   Answers will vary. Here is one possible answer for each category:
Some scientists think that turtles may use magnetic forces and smell to find their way.
Turtles lay their eggs in the sand to keep them warm.
Of every 1,000 Atlantic green, baby turtles hatched, only 1 or 2 will survive.

Page 44
1   Answers will vary. Here is one possible answer: *From the deck of a boat because plankton can't live as far down as the trench.*
2   Answers will vary. Here is one possible answer: *No, because whales do not go so far down that you would need a sea probe.*
3   More than 10,000 feet, probably closer to 11,000 feet, according to the diagram.
4   35,000 ft

Page 45–46
Story Element Planning Chart graphic organizer: Answers will vary, but students should at least partially complete the organizer and should put story elements in the correct box.

Page 48
Answers will vary. Students may list words such as the following: People in front of the camera—actors, star, main character, supporting actors, stunt people, stand-in, stunt double, crowds, animal characters, hero, villain. People off screen—director, assistant director, assistant producer, camera operators, lighting crew, electrician, stagehands, best boy, makeup artist, wardrobe mistress, property master, continuity, special effects, runners, nurse, teacher for child actors. Filming and recording equipment—cameras, booms, baffles, tracks for cameras. Other equipment—computers, carpenter's tools, electrician's tools, sound effects equipment, clapper board. Non-film essentials—water, changing rooms, cars, telephones.

Page 49
1   cameras
2   lights
3   actors
4   trucks
5   films
6   extras
7   wishes
8   waltzes
9   tomatoes
10 cities
11 thieves
12 halves

Page 50
The first word is the word that should be underlined as incorrect. The second word is the correct form of the plural.
1   foots, feet
2   mediums, media
3   plier, pliers
4   sheeps, sheep
5   trouts, trout
6   wheats, wheat
7   Correct

Page 51
1   prewrapped
2   nonprofit
3   postscript
4   prearranged
5   nonbinding
6   nonstick

Page 52
1   precut, sliced beforehand
2   preteen, possible definition: before reaching the teen years; postteen, possible definition: after 19
3   nonprint, possible definition: not printed
4   predate, possible definition: coming before or dated before; postdate, possible definition: coming after or dated later
5   posttrial, possible definition: after a trial; pretrial, possible definition: before a trial
6   nondairy
7   pregame
8   preholiday
9   postcolonial
10 noncontagious

Page 54
1   B
2   F; You may have to wait all day to audition, so you should bring a packed lunch, snacks, and bottled water.
3   B; Because the ad calls for boys up to the age of 14 only and says that they must have specific training, beyond just singing in the school chorus.
4   Students should write the following: Date: Saturday, June 20. Time: 9 a.m. Place: Westside High School. To sign legal forms and prove age, bring a parent or guardian; proof of your age, either a passport or birth certificate along with your most recent report card. Wear comfortable clothes and shoes, suitable for school; dancers should bring a leotard, tights, ballet slippers, and pointe shoes. Do not wear make-up or costumes. Also bring a packed lunch, snacks, and water.

Page 55
1   two, to, too
2   merry, marry
3   fourth, forth
4   overdo
5   overdue
6   dye
7   die
8   do
9   due, dew

Page 56
1   screen, screen
2   mouse, mouse
3   menu, menu
4   keyboard, keyboard
5   scroll, Scroll
6   windows, windows
7   port, port

Page 59
1   C
2   Answers will vary. Answers should include the notion of timing and sound and pictures working together. Here is one possible answer: *Setting the timing so that the sound and the moving images work together "in sync," so that when people talk, the words fit their lip movements.*
3   B
4   Answers will vary, but answers should contain a reason, even a simple one. For example: I would like to be a producer because I would be in charge of everything, even the money.
5   Answers will vary, but answers should include a reason.

Page 63
1   A
2   H
3   They trained animals.
4   Answers will vary, but should include the cause, which is Myrna's getting in the pink dye so that she can't appear in the film, and the effect, which is that Asta gets to be in the film instead of Myrna.

Page 64
1   10:00 p.m.
2   *101 Spotted Dogs and Striped Cats.* Answers will vary, but here is one possible answer: the theater offers a family discount for children under five and the last showing is at 5:30 in the afternoon.
3   three hours and 45 minutes
4   *Gone with the Tide*
5   *In a Galaxy Not Too Far Away*

Pages 65–66

In their comparisons, students should point out similarities and differences. They should include an introduction that states in general the main idea of their comparison, and they should also include some sort of conclusion.

Page 68

Answers will vary. Students may list ideas and subtopics such as the following: How Trains Work: computer-operated trains, electric trains, high-speed trains, steam trains. History of Trains: invention of the train, early trains, subway trains. How We Use Trains: trains in wartime, trains for long-distance travel, trains for short-distance travel, freight trains. Train Equipment: tracks, signals, stations, cars, engines, computers, ticket machines. People Who Work on Trains: conductor, driver, ticket seller, track repair team, mechanic, scheduler.

Page 69

1   marries, marrying, married, X
2   obeys, obeying, obeyed, obeyer
3   worries, worrying, worried, worrier
4   copies, copying, copied, copier
5   fries, frying, fried, fryer
6   delays, delaying, delayed, delayer
7   employs, employing, employed, employer
8   supplies, supplying, supplied, supplier
9   cries, crying, cried, crier

Page 70

1   damaging
2   stored
3   competing
4   likeable or likable
5   cutest
6   courageous
7   tying
8   eyed

Page 71

1   visitor
2   driver
3   cleaner
4   sticker
5   conductor
6   professor
7   survivor
8   auditor
9   poster

Page 72

Answers will vary. Here are some possible answers: heavier, heavily; buying, buyer; keyed, keying; prying, pries, pried, prier; hurried, hurrying, hurriedly; sadly, sadness; unites, united, uniting; carer, careful, careless, caring, cared, cares; completed, completes, completing, completion, completer; damaged, damages, damaging, damager; investor, invests, investing, invested, investment; visitor, visits, visiting, visited; governor, government, governance, governess, governed, governing; inventor, invention, invents, inventing, invented; joyous, joyless, joyful; appearance, appeared, appearing, appears; performance, performer, performing, performed, performs; actor, acted, acts, acting, action; noisy, noises, noisily; disagreement, disagreed, disagreeing, disagrees

Page 74

1   A
2   H
3   No, because the announcement says "Please turn off all cell phones and CD players."
4   No. The announcement says you have to change trains at Treasure Island if you are going to Camelot.
5   D
6   Answers will vary but should be similar to the following answer: You must have your ticket ready in order to show it to the conductor to prove you have paid your train fare.

Page 75

1   rose
2   cheap
3   earn
4   fowl
5   fur
6   toe
7   cruise
8   groan
9   maize
10 sleigh
11 soar
12 son

Page 76

Car: Answers may include road, freeway, lane, expressway, toll, turnpike, seat belt, map, road signs, windshield, tires, trunk.

Bus: Answers may include tickets, tokens, bell, window, bus stop, bus shelter, route.

Subway: Answers may include track, platform, map, station, stops, lines, standing room, doors, windows, elevator, escalator, ticket machine.

Train: Answers may include engineer, conductor, ticket counter, ticket machine, route, platform, fare, luggage, luggage racks, dining car, snack cart or trolley.

Plane: Answers may include co-pilot, steward or stewardess, departure lounge, duty free shop, luggage cart, baggage check in, flight number, destination, seat number, emergency exit, terminal, boarding pass.

Boat: Answers may include starboard, bow, first mate, crew, lifeboat, lifejackets, sail, motor, harbor, gangplank, knots.

Pages 78–79

1   D
2   F
3   Answers will vary, but the answer should contain the following logical reasoning: The poem says the sun comes up behind the train and that it is headed for the sea, where it will stop, so we know it is going west, to the west coast of whatever country it is crossing.
4   breaks
5   grown
6   lit
7   driver
8   Answers will vary. Here is one possible answer: *I would show the birds flying up out of the trees and over the train as it whizzed past.*
9   Sketches will vary.
10 Retellings will vary but should include the same events as the original poem.

Page 83

1   B
2   H
3   Men and horses pushed or pulled them.
4   J
5   A

Page 84

1   B
2   J
3   B

Pages 85–86

Students should list two places in their chart. Make sure the steps are in the correct order. Directions will vary but should be clear and orderly.

Page 88

Answers and drawings will vary.

Page 89

1   b plumber
2   b debt
3   g gnaw
4   g sign
5   h hour
6   h rhyme
7   k knit
8   l could
9   l half
10 l yolk
11 n column
12 k know
13 w whole
14 w wrong

Page 90

1   g ghost
2   d handsome
3   gh thought

4   p cupboard
5   u build
6   p pterodactyl
7   gh daughter
8   h rhinoceros
9   b subtle
10   s island
11   t listen
12   t depot
13   w answer
14   ch yacht
15   c science
16   l should

Page 91

Answers may vary, but the synonyms supplied should have almost the same meaning as the word and the possible answer listed below. Antonyms may also be different words but should definitely be opposite in meaning to the numbered word.

1   yell
2   sharp
3   catch
4   cry
5   whole
6   cold
7   find
8   hard
9   Sentences will vary but should include a synonym from the synonym column.
10   Sentences will vary but should include an antonym from the antonym column.

Page 92

Words may be listed in any order, as long as the pairs are together in the correct category. The synonyms are present/gift, anger/rage, fetch/bring, surprise/amaze. The antonyms are right/wrong, plain/fancy, buy/sell, friend/enemy.

Page 94

Answers will vary, but students should identify the people specified below, and answers should contain the key ideas of the sample answers given below.
1   Tony is the two-year-old son of Aunt Louise, and he is Cal and Jenny's cousin. The narrator tells us who Tony is.
2   Tony shares his ice cream cone with them. He gives Dan a lick, then he gives Daisy a lick, then he takes a lick. Cal describes this to Jenny.
3   Cal and Jenny take Tony in the lake to wash the ice cream off him. Cal tells Aunt Louise that he and Jenny will take him in and wash him off.
4   A speedboat creates waves when it zooms into the swimming area of the lake. The narrator recounts that event.
5   The two golden retriever dogs, Dan and Daisy, pull Tony from the lake and save him. The narrator explains what Cal and Jenny have already suggested in their speeches.

Page 95

1   raise
2   effect
3   whether
4   disapproves
5   except

Page 96

Students may put some words in more than one column, as long as the placement is logical. The following gives the most logical groupings of the words. Words to do with **measuring and recording:** barometer, wind direction, wind speed, air pressure, thermometer, temperature, Celsius, Farhrenheit, inches of rainfall, degree, hours of sunshine. Words for **types of weather conditions:** cloud, wind direction, rain, thunderstorm, sleet, snow, frost, fog, hail, drought, humidity. Words for **natural processes that affect or cause the weather:** condensation, cloud, air current, air pressure, evaporation, humidity.

Page 98

1   A
2   H
3   D
4   Answers will vary, but answers should contain logical reasons. Here are some possible answers: *Farmers need to know when to water crops, when it will be dry so they can plough, and when to harvest crops before a rainy spell. They also need to know when to expect a hot spell so they can give animals extra water and a shady place. Sailors need to know when to expect storms and other extreme weather like hurricanes and typhoons. They also need to know about wind speed and direction if their ships are sailboats.*
5   Answers will vary. Here are some possible answers: *Gardeners need to know when a drought or a long hot spell is expected so they know to water their plants. People who plan outdoor events, like concerts, sports events, or plays, need to be prepared with umbrellas and walkways that don't get muddy. People who build buildings need to know about high winds. Airports and airplane crews need to know about weather conditions.*

Pages 102–103

1   C
2   H
3   A
4   G
5   D
6   H

7   B
8   F
9   Answers will vary, but the answer should contain the key details that the shoes button up, and the clothes are very old-fashioned. The girls' swimming costumes look like sailor suits and include cloth caps, like shower caps. The boy's costume has a tank top over long shorts that look sort of like cycling shorts, but they are striped.
10   Answers will vary, but answers should mention the following: He reasons that the digital clock must be broken and the clock with hands has been put up as a temporary replacement. As for the newspaper, he thinks it must be a replica, like those you can order from newspaper companies with a facsimile of a particular date in history.

Page 104

1   Swimmer D
2   Swimmer C
3   A
4   G

Page 105–106

Students should list races at the top. In the chart, students should provide answers to the five questions. Encourage students to add at least a few words in the columns headed "Other Details" and "Things to Add in Later Paragraphs" as this will help them learn to plan their writing in advance. The newspaper article should have a lead paragraph that answers the five questions. Strong lead sentences that hook the reader should be praised, as should any imaginative or descriptive details that writers have included in the news story.